D1074792

JOURNAL FOR THE STUDY OF THE OLD TESTAMENT SUPPLEMENT SERIES
88

Editors
David J.A. Clines
Philip R. Davies

BIBLE AND LITERATURE SERIES
25

General Editor
David M. Gunn

Assistant General Editor
Danna Nolan Fewell

Consultant Editors
Elizabeth Struthers Malbon
James G. Williams

Almond Press
Sheffield

THE PERSUASIVE
APPEAL OF THE
CHRONICLER

A Rhetorical Analysis

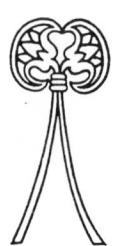

Rodney K. Duke

The Almond Press · 1990

Bible and Literature Series, 25

General Editor: David M. Gunn
(Columbia Theological Seminary, Decatur, Georgia)
Assistant General Editor: Danna Nolan Fewell
(Perkins School of Theology, Dallas, Texas)
Consultant Editors: Elizabeth Struthers Malbon
(Virginia Polytechnic Institute & State University, Blacksburg, Virginia)
James G. Williams
(Syracuse University, Syracuse, New York)

Published by Almond Press

Editorial direction: David M. Gunn
Columbia Theological Seminary
P.O. Box 520, Decatur
GA 30031, U.S.A.

Almond Press is an imprint of
Sheffield Academic Press Ltd
The University of Sheffield
343 Fulwood Road
Sheffield S10 3BP
England

Typeset by Sheffield Academic Press and
printed on acid-free paper in Great Britain
by Billing & Sons Ltd
Worcester

British Library Cataloguing in Publication Data

Duke, Rodney K.
    The persuasive appeal of the chronicler.
    1. Bible. O.T. Chronicles—Critical studies
    I. Title   II. Series
    222.606

ISSN 0260-4493
ISSN 0309-0787
ISBN 1-85075-228-1

CONTENTS

Appendix

ACKNOWLEDGMENTS

To both Robert Detweiler and Robert Paul of Emory University, I express my gratitude for expanding my horizons and introducing me to methods of literary criticism which I have brought over to my field of biblical studies. To John Hayes of Emory University and David Gunn of Columbia Theological Seminary, I am indebted for their advice and encouragement on this project.

However it is Jane, my wife and best friend, to whom I dedicate this work in acknowledgment of her inestimable support and of the great sacrifices she has made for me:

Many daughters have done nobly,
But you excel them all (Proverbs 31.29).

Chapter 1

INTRODUCTION

A. *The Objective of the Study*

In this book the books of Chronicles are analyzed and described from a rhetorical perspective. The analysis focuses on Chronicles as a whole rather than on any particular unit within the work. As a result the observations made are panoramic and provisional rather than microscopic and categorical. As such this book may serve as a prolegomenon to more detailed rhetorical readings of Chronicles.

The purposes of this introductory chapter are to identify the place of the rhetorical approach of this study within the trends of Chronicles research, to identify the methodological presuppositions and working hypotheses employed herein, and to introduce the particular type of rhetorical approach utilized.

B. *The Place of this Study in Chronicles Research*

1. *Major Trends in Chronicles Research*

The dominant questions of critical biblical research regarding the books of Chronicles have revolved around historical concerns. Attention has focused primarily on their value as a historical record. The presence of discrepancies between the account in Chronicles of the history of Judah and the account in Samuel–Kings has been leveled as an indictment against the veracity of Chronicles by some and harmonized or argued away by others. Some have maintained that the composer/s utilized ancient and reliable sources; others have countered with the charge that the composer/s created a piece of fraudulent fiction. A secondary focus has been on literary-historical questions of date, authorship, purpose, message, internal unity, and relationship to Ezra–Nehemiah. To date scholars have not arrived at a consensus regarding these issues.

a. *Prior to the Nineteenth Century*

With some exceptions, the historicity of Chronicles prompted little debate prior to the nineteenth century. In fact, the books of Chronicles generally evoked little attention. Although some difficult areas of interpretation were recognized, the general reliability of the books was largely taken for granted, particularly within the Christian Church.

Among Jewish scholars, prior to the medieval period, Chronicles occupied a minor place. Difficulties in the genealogical lists were recognized. Rabbis tended to reserve the genealogies, and indeed the whole work, for scholarly use rather than liturgical or popular use.[1] Medieval Jewish scholars such as Rashi (1040–1105), David Kimchi (c. 1160–1235), and Gersonides (1288–c. 1344), adhered closely to the literal meaning of the text of Chronicles and gave its historical worth a high appraisal.[2]

Although most of the Christian Fathers ignored Chronicles or treated it peripherally, Jerome extravagantly praised the book and its value.[3] Whether or not his assessment rested on a historical or an allegorical interpretation cannot be demonstrated since his commentary is not extant. However, in the commentaries of Theodoret of Cyrrhus (c. 393–458), Procopius of Gaza (c. 475–538), and Rabanus Maurus (c. 776–856), all who viewed the book as a guide for godly action, the historical reliability is never questioned, but rather assumed.[4] On the whole, medieval commentators tended to be harmonistic when regarding the differences that exist between the accounts in Samuel–Kings and in Chronicles, and acted on the premise that its historical veracity was unimpugnable.[5]

---

[1] R.O. Rigsby, 'The Historiography of Speeches and Prayers in the Books of Chronicles' (Th.D. dissertation; Southern Baptist Theological Seminary, 1973), p. 4; T. Willi, *Die Chronik als Auslegung* (FRLANT, 106; Göttingen: Vandenhoeck & Ruprecht, 1972), pp. 13, 16.

[2] Rigsby, p. 4; Willi, pp. 20-21.

[3] Rigsby, pp. 5-6.

[4] *Ibid.*, pp. 6-7.

[5] *Ibid.*, p. 7.

With the development of the historical perspective of the Renaissance, foundations were laid for a reversal of this view. Joseph Solomon Delmedigo (1591–1655), a Jewish scholar, questioned whether Chronicles should be regarded as an interpretation rather than as a narrative. He supported this designation on the grounds that Chronicles was composed at a time far removed from the events described, a conclusion he deduced from the genealogies.[1] Baruch de Spinoza (1632–1677), perhaps influenced by Delmedigo, utilized a comparison of the genealogies in 1 Chronicles 9 and Nehemiah to support his conclusion that the books of Chronicles were written after the time of Ezra, and possible after the restoration of the temple by Judas Maccabaeus.[2] Although stating that he did not 'aim at disparaging their authority', he expressed his astonishment that these books were included in the canon when others were excluded as apocryphal.[3]

b. *Nineteenth Century*
(1) *The Historical Reliability of Chronicles and Pentateuchal Criticism*
In regard to the books of Chronicles, one can summarize the nineteenth century as a period of vigorous debate over the historical reliability of Chronicles. Prior to the initiation of this debate, the scholarly consensus regarding Chronicles was represented by J.G. Eichhorn, in his *Einleitung in das Alte Testament* (1780–82, 3rd edn 1803). There he offered a critical explanation of the use of sources by the author of Chronicles, whom he believed to have been Ezra.[4] He theorized that the author drew on some canonical works as well as on other ancient histories, genealogies and records, some of which had been preserved by temple personnel.[5] Material parallel and

[1] Willi, pp. 24-25.
[2] Baruch de Spinoza, *The Chief Works of Benedict de Spinoza* (trans. R.H.M. Elwes; vol. 1: *Theologico-Political Treatise*; George Bell and Sons, 1883; reprint edn, New York: Dover, 1951), 1.146. Willi (p. 29) discusses the possible connection between Delmedigo and Spinoza.
[3] Spinoza, 1.146.
[4] J.G. Eichhorn, *Einleitung in das Alte Testament* (3 vols.; 3rd edn; Leipzig: Weidmann, 1803), 2.579-601.
[5] *Ibid.*, 2.589.

verbally similar to the account in Samuel–Kings was explained by the use of common sources rather than by dependence on those books, although Eichhorn believed that the Chronicler also knew and cited the canonical Samuel.[1] Differences within parallel material was accounted for by the theses that scribal inaccuracies had entered into some of the sources unused by the author before he compiled them, and that the author adapted these sources orthographically, theologically, and culturally as he used and abridged them.[2] Assuming the sources to be reliable and the author to be a careful compiler, Eichhorn afforded Chronicles a high degree of accuracy.[3]

W.M.L. de Wette (1790–1849) sharply criticized the view of Eichhorn in his *Beiträge zur Einleitung in das Alte Testament* (1806–1807), a work which initiated a decisive turn in Chronicles research.[4] The first volume, and most significant one for Chronicles research, is notably entitled *Kritischer Versuch über die Glaubwürdigkeit der Bücher der Chronik mit Hinsicht auf die Geschichte der Mosaischen Bücher und Gesetzgebung: Ein Nachtrag zu den Vaterschen Untersuchungen über den Pentateuch.* To place de Wette's work on Chronicles in its proper context, one should recall that the burning issue of the nineteenth century was the history of the composition of the Pentateuch. De Wette's investigation into the reliability of Chronicles was directed towards this goal. Since Chronicles at face value supported claims to the early existence of the Mosaic books and cultic institutions, a claim de Wette did not find supported in the Former Prophets, the question of the reliability of Chronicles became bound to the investigation of the date and reliability of the Pentateuch and

---

[1] *Ibid.*, 2.590-91.
[2] *Ibid.*, 2.587-89.
[3] *Ibid.*, 2.599-600.
[4] W.M.L. de Wette, *Beiträge zur Einleitung in das Alte Testament* (2 vols.; Halle: Schimmelpfennig, vol. 1, 1806, vol. 2, 1807). For a fuller summary of the contribution of de Wette see M.P. Graham, 'The Utilization of 1 and 2 Chronicles in the Reconstruction of the Israelite History in the Nineteenth Century' (Ph.D. dissertation, Emory University, 1983), pp. 14-60.

vice versa. And, if one record was not reliable, then neither was the other.[1]

In the first volume of the *Beiträge* de Wette argued, contrary to Eichhorn, that where the author had material in common with Samuel–Kings, the author had depended on those canonical books as his source; but where the material was different, one could find no evidence that it was based on reliable historical sources.[2] Rather, he suggested that the Chronicler was responsible for the unique material on the grounds that the work bears throughout the impress of one individual.[3] This variant material de Wette regarded as 'Änderungen, Zusätze, und Verfälschungen' ('alterations, additions, and falsifications').[4] De Wette further argued that, when the two accounts were compared, the account in Samuel–Kings was older, preserved a superior report, was compiled more carefully, and had fewer mythical elaborations. Chronicles, on the other hand, showed biases for the tribe of Levi, for the Judean cult, for the nation of Judah, and against the Northern Kingdom.[5] Therefore, because of

---

[1] De Wette raised this connection between the authenticity of the Pentateuch and the reliability of Chronicles in his introductory remarks in the first volume (1.7-9), spent the second half of this volume noting the consequences of his conclusions regarding Chronicles ('Resultate für die Geschichte der Mosaischen Bücher und Gesetzgebung', 1.133-299), and devoted 'Part One' of the second volume to a 'Kritik der Mosaischen Geschichte'. See Graham, pp. 57-59, for a summary of de Wette's contributions to the development of the documentary hypothesis as it came to its later expression by J. Wellhausen.

[2] De Wette, 1.10-41.

[3] *Ibid.*, 1.60-61.

[4] *Ibid.*, 1.61, note.

[5] *Ibid.*, 1.42-132. De Wette granted the superiority of the account of Samuel–Kings over Chronicles. However, he did not believe the former sufficient for reconstructing the political history of Israel either, although he did use it for reconstructing Israel's religious history (de Wette, 1.225, and see Graham, pp. 55-57). Still, de Wette's comparison of Chronicles to Samuel–Kings had a great impact on how the two works were treated. Prior to de Wette, scholars harmonized the accounts of the Former Prophets and Chronicles, regarding them relatively equally. After the work of de Wette, most scholars tended to hold the Former Prophets up as the standard for comparison, regarding the narrative in Samuel–Kings as more accurate and the the narrative of Chronicles as more tendentious. When discrepancies were dis-

Chronicles' falsifications and tendentiousness, de Wette declared the work to be without any historical value. He concluded his investigation into the reliability of Chronicles with the remark:

> (Why should we make the effort to save a credibility which is already lost?—Enough, I allow the contradiction to stand and lay it on the tendentiousness and inauthenticity of Chronicles.)[1]

De Wette's work initiated a major debate over the reliability of Chronicles, a debate which belonged to the larger context of Pentateuchal criticism and the reconstruction of the history of Israel's cult. Two scholars who early supported and furthered the major points of de Wette's work were W. Gesenius (1815) and K.W.P. Gramberg (1823).[2] This side of the debate, believing that the author of Chronicles had only canonical works as sources, portrayed the author as a creative writer who maliciously or otherwise contrived a fictional history. Their arguments were met by counter-arguments from such scholars as J.G. Dahler (1819), C.F. Keil (1833), F.K. Movers (1834), and H.A.C. Haevernick (1839).[3] In defence of the historical reliability of Chronicles (as well as the early date of the Pentateuch and its portrayal of the cult) this second group of scholars produced detailed explanations and harmonizations for the

covered between the two narratives, it was the account in Chronicles which had to be explained or rejected. See S. Japhet, 'The Historical Reliability of Chronicles', *JSOT* 33 (1985), pp. 85-86.

1 'Warum sollen wir uns hier die Mühe geben, eine Glaubswürdigkeit zu retten, die schon verloren ist?—Genug, ich lasse den Widerspruch, und schiebe ihn auf die Partheilichkeit und Unächtheit der Chronik' (de Wette, 1.132).

2 W. Gesenius, *Geschichte der hebräischen Sprache und Schrift* (Leipzig: Friedrich Christian Wilhelm Vogel, 1815; reprint edn, Hildesheim: Georg Olms, 1973), pp. 37-44; K.P.W. Gramberg, *Die Chronik* (Halle: Eduard Anton, 1823).

3 J.G. Dahler, *De librorum paralipomenon auctoritate atque fide historica disputat* (Argentorati: Johannis Henrici Heitz, 1819); cited in Graham, pp. 79-95; C.F. Keil, *Apologetischer Versuch über die Bücher der Chronik und über die Integrität des Buches Esra* (Berlin: Ludwig Oehmigke, 1833); F.K. Movers, *Kritische Untersuchungen über die biblische Chronik* (Bonn: T. Habricht, 1834); H.A.C. Haevernick, *Handbuch der historisch-kritischen Einleitung in das Alte Testament* (Erlangen: Cark Heyder, 1839), 2.174-278. For a synopsis of the contribution of Dahler, Keil, Movers and Haevernick, see Graham, pp. 76-95.

apparent discrepancies, maintained that Chronicles shared a common source with Samuel–Kings and/or used other reliable sources, and argued that the account in Chronicles differed from that of Samuel–Kings because it focused on different subject matter. For them, the Chronicler was a biased but accurate and well-intentioned compiler of accurate ancient records.

For the first three-fourths of the nineteenth century biblical historians reacted moderately to this initial debate, following neither of the extreme positions represented by de Wette and Keil. They continued to use Chronicles as a source for reconstructing the history of Israel, admitting that it contained distortions, but believing that reliable information could be separated from the unreliable.[1]

A second wave of support for de Wette's position was launched in the 1860s and 1870s. Just as de Wette's argument for the unreliability of Chronicles had accompanied the thesis for the late date of the Pentateuch, in a similar manner the renewed case against the historicity of Chronicles accompanied arguments supporting a late date for the Priestly Document of the Pentateuch.[2] Although the scholars in this second wave came to varying conclusions regarding the sources and the motives of the Chronicler, they gravitated toward de Wette's conclusion regarding the unreliability of Chronicles as a source for historical reconstruction. Participating in this second movement were such scholars as K.H. Graf (1866), J.W. Colenso (1862-79), J. Wellhausen (1878), and W. Vatke (1886).[3]

---

[1] Graham, pp. 96-198.

[2] Japhet, 'Reliability', pp. 84-88; Graham, pp. 199-325.

[3] K.H. Graf, *Die geschichtlichen Bücher des Alten Testaments* (Leipzig: T.O. Weigel, 1866), second part, 'Das Buch der Chronik als Geschichtsquelle', pp. 114-247; J.W. Colenso, *The Pentateuch and the Book of Joshua Critically Examined* (5 vols.; London: Longman, Green, Longman, Robert & Green, 1862-79), part 7, pp. 304-89; J. Wellhausen, *Prolegomena zur Geschichte Israels* (Berlin: Reimer, 1883), originally published in 1878 as the first volume of Wellhausen's *Geschichte Israels*; citations are from *Prolegomena to the History of Ancient Israel*, a translation of the 2nd edn of 1883 (Edinburgh: A. & C. Black, 1885; Cleveland: World, 1957); W. Vatke, *Historisch-kritische Einleitung in das Alte Testament* (ed. H.G.S. Preiss; Bonn: Emil

With Wellhausen's *Prolegomena* (1878), the late date of P was popularized and de Wette's position regarding Chronicles was restated. Wellhausen supported the thesis that whereas Samuel–Kings portrayed Israelite history as revised according to the perspective of Deuteronomy, Chronicles evaluated and idealized the past according the perspective of the Pentateuchal law in general and the Priestly Code in particular.[1] He, too spoke of Chronicles' historical worth in pejorative terms: 'We have before us a deliberate and in its motives a very transparent mutilation of the original narrative as preserved for us in the Book of Samuel',[2] 'complete and manifest contradiction',[3] 'by distorting and mutilating his original',[4] 'it is only the tradition of the older source that possesses historical value'.[5]

As a result of the renewed debate, histories of Israel produced during the last quarter of this century tended to fall into two groups. Those who followed the late dating of P generally treated the historical picture in Chronicles with great suspicion. The majority of these scholars rejected Chronicles as a source for reconstruction of the pre-exilic period. In contrast, those who supported a pre-exilic date for P generally held a greater confidence in the historical reliability of Chronicles and did use data unique to Chronicles in their reconstructions.[6]

(2) *The Impact of Archaeology and Ancient Near Eastern Research*
Although there existed extreme views regarding the reliability of Chronicles, one also finds a tendency toward more moderate assessments. This tendency appears to have been given impetus by some complementary shifts in the major concerns of biblical scholars toward the end of the nineteenth century.

Strauss, 1886), pp. 471-82. For a review of this second wave of support, see Graham, pp. 199-325.
[1] Wellhausen, pp. 171-72, 189-90, 294.
[2] *Ibid.*, p. 173.
[3] *Ibid.*, p. 176.
[4] *Ibid.*
[5] *Ibid.*, p. 182.
[6] Graham, pp. 256-323.

This century saw the growth and development of archaeology as a discipline. To some degree this development heightened the debate. Scholars such as George Rawlinson, Eberhard Schrader, and Archibald H. Sayce attempted to use the new archaeological data apologetically to disprove the theories of 'higher criticism', and to defend the unique data in Chronicles.[1] Their arguments were countered by W.R. Smith, S.R. Driver, Thomas K. Cheyne and others who rather successfully pointed out that archaeological data generally neither proved nor disproved such theories.[2] However, the development of archaeology also helped to reshape the earlier debate. The interest of some scholars began to shift away from reconstructing the history of composition of the Pentateuch and the history of the religion of Israel to reconstructing the world of the ancient Near East.[3] Scholars began to focus on the biblical literature, including the books of Chronicles, as written historical sources to be used in a complementary fashion with archaeological data to give a fuller picture of ancient history.[4] One of those representing this trend was Hugo Winckler

[1] G. Rawlinson, *The Historical Evidences of the Truth of the Scripture Records* (Bampton Lecture, 1859; London: John Murray, 1859), esp. pp. 113-55, and *Ezra and Nehemiah* (Men of the Bible; New York: Fleming H. Revell, 1890), esp. pp. 54-59; E. Schraeder, *Die Keilschriften und das Alte Testament* (Giessen: J. Ricker, 1872; ET *The Cuneiform Inscriptions and the Old Testament*, 2 vols.; trans. from 2nd edn by O.C. Whitehouse; London: Williams and Norgate, 1885, 1888), esp. 1.xxii-xxiv and 2.52-59; and A.H. Sayce, *Fresh Light from the Ancient Monuments* (By-Paths of Bible Knowledge, 3 [later changed to 2]; London: The Religious Tract Society, 1883), and *The 'Higher Criticism' and the Verdict of the Monuments* (2nd edn; London: SPCK, 1894 [1893]), esp. pp. 457-68. For a discussion of the contribution of these works, see Graham, pp. 339-76.

[2] W.R. Smith, *The Old Testament in the Jewish Church* (2nd edn; London: A. & C. Black, 1892; reprinted edn, 1908), esp. pp. 140-48; S.R. Driver, 'Hebrew Authority', *Authority and Archaeology: Sacred and Profane* (ed. David G. Hogarth; New York: Charles Scribner's Sons, 1899), pp. 143-51; and T.K. Cheyne, *The Decline and Fall of the Kingdom of Judah* (London: A. & C. Black, 1908), esp. part I, pp. 3-95, on the use of Kings and Chronicles for historical reconstruction, and pp. 3-7 for his evaluation of Chronicles. For further evaluation of these works, see Graham, pp. 377-408.

[3] Japhet, 'Reliability', pp. 90-91.

[4] *Ibid.*

(1892).[1] Rather than totally rejecting Chronicles as a historical source, he believed that each case of unique material in
Chronicles, which did not reveal the influence of the Chronicler's biases, needed to be carefully re-examined for relevant
historical data.[2] Another mediating position, reflecting a complementary
shift, is represented by Theodore G. Soares's article, 'The
Import of the Chronicles as a Piece of Religio-Historical Literature' (1899).[3] Soares acknowledged a difference in ancient
and modern historiography and even looked for changes in
historiographical style in the Old Testament. He presented five
principles of the Chronicler's historiography by which he
sought to explain how the Chronicler utilized his existing
material in different ways in order to accomplish his objective.[4] Unlike the extreme positions, which regarded the
Chronicler either as a careful compiler or a malicious author

[1] H. Winckler, 'Bemerkungen zur Chronik als Geschichtsquelle',
Alttestamentliche Untersuchungen (Leipzig: Eduard Pfeiffer, 1892),
pp. 157-67.
[2] Winckler actually took his cue from Graf who had recognized that
buried under the Chronicler's biased presentation lay some historical
kernels not found in Samuel–Kings (pp. 157-58; see Graf, pp. 138-39,
187). W.E. Barnes ('The Midrashic Element in Chronicles', *Expositor*
fifth series, 4 [1896], pp. 434-37), although still cautious about accepting
details expressed in the Chronicler's phraseology, also cautioned
about rejecting the substance of a story which showed his *Tendenz*. In
defense, he pointed out how the account of Jehoiada's revolution in 2
Chronicles 23 reveals the same criteria which had been applied to
reject such material as fiction, yet the account is credited with factual
value because it also occurs in the parallel narrative of 2 Kings 11.
[3] T.G. Soares, 'The Import of the Chronicles as a Piece of Religio-Historical Literature', *AJT* 3 (1899), pp. 251-74. Rigsby pointed out the shift
in perspective represented by Soares, pp. 21-22.
[4] The five principles Soares identified are: (1) Wherever the Chronicler was acting as a historian and giving facts, he compiled from his
sources. (2) When he wanted to convey a religious teaching already
conveyed by the same narrative in a source, he compiled. (3) When the
message his source conveyed did not exactly suit his purpose, he partly
compiled and partly rewrote. (4) When his source recorded an event in
a brief historical manner but did not convey the religious teaching, he
generally rewrote history. (5) In the great periods of the history and for
critical events, he discarded the compilatory method and sought his
own style to present a picture of the past with a message to his contemporaries (Soares, p. 254).

of fiction, Soares portrayed the Chronicler as a sincere author of a history who also had nonhistorical teaching objectives.[1]

(3) *Relationship of Chronicles to Ezra–Nehemiah*

Prior to the nineteenth century, Ezra had traditionally been identified as the author both of the book of Ezra and of most of the books of Chronicles.[2] The question of the relationship of Chronicles to Ezra–Nehemiah came under the scrutiny of L. Zunz[3] in 1832 and of F.K. Movers in 1834, independently of one another. Both reached similar conclusions. Movers connected the author/compiler of Chronicles with much of Ezra.[4] Zunz traced the work of the author of Chronicles through both Ezra and Nehemiah. He concluded, however, that the author of Chronicles was not Ezra, but, to the contrary, the author of these works was the 'Chronicler'.[5] This theory grew in popularity until it became virtually axiomatic.[6] As a result, the evaluation of the historical reliability of these books became inextricably tied together. Again, extreme positions regarding their historicity may be found. C.C. Torrey argued that much of Ezra–Nehemiah was really the creative composition of the Chronicler and concluded that it had no value as a history of the Jews in the Persian period.[7] E. Meyer, on the other hand, concluding that the Aramaic portions of Ezra were authentic documents from reliable sources, ascribed a high historical value to Ezra–Nehemiah.[8]

---

[1] So, too, similarly concluded W.E. Barnes, who also examined the Chronicler's style (Barnes, pp. 426-39).

[2] Japhet, 'Reliability', p. 88.

[3] L. Zunz, *Die gottesdienstlichen Vorträge der Juden historisch entwickelt* (Berlin: A. Asher, 1832; reprint edn, Hildesheim: Georg Olms, 1966), pp. 13-36.

[4] Movers, pp. 11-14.

[5] Japhet, 'Reliability', p. 88.

[6] S. Japhet, 'The Supposed Common Authorship of Chronicles and Ezra–Nehemiah Investigated Anew', *VT* 18 (1968), pp. 330-33.

[7] C.C. Torrey, *The Composition and Historical Value of Ezra–Nehemiah* (Giessen: J. Ricker, 1896), pp. 4-65. His basic conclusions were re-enforced and further argued in his *Ezra Studies* (Chicago: University of Chicago, 1910).

[8] E. Meyer, *Die Entstehung des Judenthums* (Halle: Max Niemeyer, 1896), pp. 8-71.

c. *Twentieth Century*

(1) *Continued Trends*

As the issue of dating the Pentateuchal 'documents' lost some of its centrality in the twentieth century, the importance of the books of Chronicles to this debate lessened and this work was increasingly studied more in its own right.[1] Questions about its history of composition, purpose and setting grew in importance. Still, the various issues, approaches, and conclusions found in the nineteenth century regarding Chronicles remained representative of much of the discussion in the twentieth century.

The discussion over the sources of Chronicles and over its historical reliability continued with evaluations covering the whole range of the spectrum. Some scholars totally rejected Chronicles as a historical source for the pre-exilic period: C.C. Torrey (1910), R.H. Pfeiffer (1941), and P. Welten (1973).[2] Some, while accepting a few details, generally attributed very little historical value to the work: E.L. Curtis and A.A. Madsen (1910), G.B. Gray (1913), J.E. McFadyen (1932), W.O.E. Oesterley and T.H. Robinson (1934), O. Eissfeldt (1938), M. Noth (1943), W. Rudolph (1955), T. Willi (1972), R. Mosis (1973), R. Micheel (1983).[3] Others, while exercising much

---

[1] Japhet, 'Reliability', p. 96.

[2] Torrey, *Ezra Studies* (Torrey also rejected most of Ezra–Nehemiah for reconstructing the Persian period as well); R.H. Pfeiffer, *Introduction to the Old Testament* (New York: Harper & Brothers, 1941). P. Welten, *Geschichte und Geschichtsdarstellung in den Chronikbüchern* (WMANT, 42; Neukirchen-Vluyn: Neukirchener Verlag, 1973).

[3] E.L. Curtis and A.A. Madsen, *A Critical and Exegetical Commentary on the Books of Chronicles* (ICC; New York: Charles Scribner's Sons, 1910); G.B. Gray, *A Critical Introduction to the Old Testament* (New York: Charles Scribner's Sons, 1913); J.E. McFadyen, *Introduction to the Old Testament* (London: Hodder & Stoughton, 1932); W.O.E. Oesterley and T.H. Robinson, *An Introduction to the Books of the Old Testament* (London: SPCK, 1934; Cleveland: World, 1958); O. Eissfeldt, *The Old Testament: An Introduction* (3rd edn; trans. P.R. Ackroyd; Oxford: Basil Blackwell, 1965; New York: Harper & Row, 1976 [1st German edn, 1938]); M. Noth, *Überlieferungsgeschichtliche Studien* (Wiesbaden-Biebrich: Becker, 1943; reprint edn, Tübingen: Max Niemeyer, 1957); W. Rudolph, *Chronikbücher* (HAT, 21; Tübingen: J.C.B. Mohr [Paul Siebeck], 1955); Willi, *Die Chronik als Auslegung*; R. Mosis, *Untersuchungen zur Theologie des chronistischen*

caution, held the unique tradition of Chronicles in higher
regard: W.F. Albright (1950), S. Talmon (1958), J. Bright
(1959), J.M. Myers (1965), F.L. Moriarty (1965) and H.G.M.
Williamson (1982).[1] Then, too, some have gone still further in
defending the general historical genuineness of the book:
Willis J. Beecher (1915), E.J. Young (1949), Merrill F. Unger
(1951), and J. Barton Payne (1962).[2] Archaeological data was
marshalled to prove the accuracy of some of the Chronicles
sources;[3] and archaeological data was interpreted as proving
no such thing.[4]

Despite the range of final assessments regarding the general
value of Chronicles, the great majority of scholars recognized
Chronicles as a source which the historian should not neglect,
but which needed to be investigated critically. Following the
approach taken in the previous century, they continued to
examine individual units of the unique material for information not influenced by the Chronicler's biases. Such studies
were often correlated with archaeological and geographical
data in a developing historico-geographical approach to bibli-

---

Geschichtswerkes (FTS, 92; Freiburg: Herder, 1973); R. Micheel, *Die
Seher- und Prophetenüberlieferungen in der Chronik* (BET, 18;
Frankfurt am Main: Peter Lang, 1983).
[1] W.F. Albright, 'The Judicial Reform of Jehoshaphat', *Alexander
Marx Jubilee Volume* (New York: Jewish Theological Seminary of
America, 1950), pp. 61-82; S. Talmon, 'Divergences in the Calendar
Reckoning in Ephraim and Judah', *VT* 8 (1958), pp. 48-74; J. Bright, *A
History of Israel* (Philadelphia: Westminster, 1959); J.M. Meyers, *I
and II Chronicles* (Anchor Bible; Garden City, NY: Doubleday, 1965);
F.L. Moriarty, 'The Chronicler's Account of Hezekiah's Reform', *CBQ*
27 (1965), pp. 399-406; H.G.M. Williamson, *1 and 2 Chronicles* (New
Century Bible Commentary; Grand Rapids, MI: Eerdmans, 1982).
[2] W.J. Beecher, 'Chronicles, Books of', *The International Standard
Bible Encyclopaedia* (5 vols.; ed. J. Orr *et al.*; Chicago: Howard-Severance, 1915), 1.629-35; E.J. Young, *An Introduction to the Old Testament* (Grand Rapids, MI: Eerdmans, 1949; reset edn, 1958); J.B.
Payne, 'I Chronicles, II Chronicles', *The Wycliffe Bible Commentary*
(ed. C.F. Pfeiffer and E.F. Harrison; London: Oliphants, 1962).
[3] R.A.S. Macalister, 'The Craftsmen's Guild of the Tribe of Judah',
PEQ 37 (1905), pp. 243-53, 328-42; W.F. Albright, 'Judicial Reform'.
[4] R. North, 'Does Archaeology Prove Chronicles' Sources?', *A Light
unto My Path* (ed. H.N. Bream, R.D. Heim and C.A. Moore; Philadelphia: Temple University, 1974), pp. 375-401.

cal studies.[1] These studies tended to focus on topographical data, place names, genealogies, and incidental military and political details.[2]

(2) New Trends

(a) *The history of composition*. Analogous concerns and methods of nineteenth-century Pentateuchal criticism increasingly were applied to the historical books in the twentieth century.[3] Correspondingly attention turned to Chronicles' history of composition. Rudolph Kittel (1902) postulated four stages of editorial activity.[4] J.W. Rothstein and J. Haenel (1927), breaking away from the thesis that Chronicles was a Priestly writing, maintained that the book had undergone both a Priestly and a Deuteronomic recension.[5] Welch identified an original Chronicler of about 515 BCE and a later contributor.[6] M. Noth (1943), however, applying a traditio-critical

---

[1] Albrecht Alt, although not noted for contributions to research on Chronicles, is credited with establishing the historico-geographical approach to issues of Israel's history. See R.E. Clements, *One Hundred Years of Old Testament Interpretation* (Philadelphia: Westminster, 1976), p. 37.

[2] For example see: W.F. Albright, 'The Date and Personality of the Chronicler', *JBL* 40 (1921), pp. 104-24, and 'Judicial Reform' (1950); G. Beyer, 'Beiträge zur Territorialgeschichte von Südwestpalästina im Altertum', *ZDPV* 54 (1931), pp. 113-70 (see part I, 'Das Festungssystem Rehabeams', pp. 113-34); M. Noth, 'Eine siedlungsgeographische Liste in 1. Chr. 2 und 4', *ZDPV* 55 (1932), pp. 97-124; S. Talmon, 'Divergences' (1958); F.L. Moriarty (1965); R.W. Klein, 'Historical Allusions within the Genealogies', paper presented at the Annual Meeting of the Society of Biblical Literature (November 1985). See P. Welten (*Geschichte*) for a critique of the reliability of data in military-related texts.

[3] Clements, pp. 33-34.

[4] R. Kittel, *Die Bücher der Chronik und Esra, Nehemia und Esther* (HAT; Göttingen: Vandenhoeck & Ruprecht, 1902), pp. x-xvi, cited by Rigsby, p. 29.

[5] J.W. Rothstein and J. Haenel, *Kommentar zum ersten Buch der Chronik* (2 parts; KAT, 18; Leipzig: A. Deichert, 1927), 2.lix-lxix. The thesis of Deuteronomic influence was further supported by G. von Rad in *Das Geschichtsbild des chronistischen Werkes* (BWANT, 54; Stuttgart: W. Kohlhammer, 1930).

[6] A.C. Welch, *The Work of the Chronicler* (London: Oxford University Press, 1939), pp. 5-6, 146-60.

approach came to much the same evaluation as de Wette: even though there had been many additions, an Ur-Chronicles had existed which was essentially the history of Samuel–Kings but with the Chronicler's own theological, creative additions.[1] Similarly, W. Rudolph (1954), although admitting there have been several additions, does not find them to be uniform enough in nature to identify specific redactions.[2] K. Galling (1954) divided Chronicles–Ezra–Nehemiah into two continuous strata.[3] F.M. Cross has proposed a three-edition theory.[4] Ackroyd, seeing the possibilities of later additions and more than one edition, along with a flux in the textual transmission, has suggested that the literary history of Chronicles–Ezra–Nehemiah was one of continuous and ongoing formation, possibly a process with a 'school of thought', a process which was frozen at a particular point in time in the form we now have.[5] However, with the recent claim that where the Chronicler used a text of Samuel–Kings he used a 'Palestinian' text type more similar to 4QSamuel than to the one represented in the Massoretic tradition, source and traditio-historical issues have become more complex. Conclusions based on detailed textual comparisons between Chronicles and parallel passages in Samuel–Kings have been called into question.[6]

(b) *The relationship of Chronicles to Ezra–Nehemiah.* One issue, which if settled would help to illumine the historical

---

[1] Noth, *Studien*, pp. 112-22.

[2] W. Rudolph, 'Problems of the Books of Chronicles', *VT* 4 (1954), p. 402.

[3] K. Galling, *Die Bücher der Chronik, Esra, Nehemia* (Das Alte Testament Deutsch, 12; Göttingen: Vandenhoeck & Ruprecht, 1954), pp. 8-12, 14-17.

[4] F.M. Cross, 'A Reconstruction of the Judean Restoration', *JBL* 94 (1975), pp. 4-18.

[5] P.R. Ackroyd, 'The Historical Literature', *The Hebrew Bible and its Modern Interpreters* (ed. D.A. Knight and G.M. Tucker; Philadelphia: Fortress, 1985), p. 307.

[6] See the work of W.E. Lemke ('Synoptic Studies in the Chronicler's History' [Th.D. thesis; Harvard Divinity School, 1963]), who concluded that the Chronicler's *Vorlage* was of a different text type from that behind the Massoretic Text of Samuel–Kings (pp. 235-40).

issues of date, authorship and compositional history, has been raised anew this century: the relationship of Chronicles to Ezra–Nehemiah. Although, according to P.R. Ackroyd, most of modern critical scholarship still assumes a compositional unity for these books,[1] this thesis of unity has been vigorously challenged recently. D.N. Freedman (1961) noted that the Chronicler's interest in the house of David is not a significant concern in Ezra–Nehemiah except in the first few chapters of Ezra. He argued, because of the interest in David only in the first part of Ezra and because of parallels between the accounts of rebuilding the temple in Ezra and the building of the first temple in Chronicles, that Chronicles originally extended to the first part of what is now Ezra.[2] Observing that previous studies concentrated on points of similarity in language and style rather than also on the differences, Sara Japhet (1968) has explained the shared features as due to the fact that the books belong to the same general linguistic stratum. At the same time she demonstrated several linguistic differences. She concluded that Chronicles reflects a later stage of Hebrew than that of Ezra–Nehemiah.[3] Further support was added incidentally by Willi (1972), who concluded that in terms of historiographical style Chronicles was a separate work, although he still believes that they share the same author.[4] J.D. Newsome (1973) pointed to contrasting motifs and depictions as evidence that the works were composed by authors with different interests.[5] Combining some of these

[1] P.R. Ackroyd, 'Chronicles, I and II', *IDBSup* (ed. K. Crim *et al.*; Nashville: Abingdon, 1976), p. 156.
[2] D.N. Freedman, 'The Chronicler's Purpose', *CBQ* 23 (1961), pp. 436-42.
[3] Japhet, 'Authorship'. It is this writer's opinion that Japhet's linguistic evidence does indicate an opposition between Chronicles and Ezra–Nehemiah; however, her conclusion that Chronicles represents a later linguistic stratum is not sufficiently supported by the evidence. On the contrary, some of the evidence she cites (e.g. the lack of Persian loan words in Chronicles [pp. 354-57] and its preservation of the short form of the imperfect consecutive [pp. 334-41]) might point to Chronicles being earlier.
[4] Willi, pp. 176-81.
[5] J.D. Newsome, Jr, 'The Chronicler's View of Prophecy' (Ph.D. dissertation; Vanderbilt University, 1973), pp. 266-74.

approaches, H. Williamson examined the Greek versions, linguistic data, and ideological features. He, too, reached the conclusion that this variety of evidence yields the verdict that Chronicles is a separate work from Ezra–Nehemiah.[1]

(c) *Chronicles as a literary work.* Another major emphasis in Chronicles research has developed in this century, that of viewing the work also as a literary product and not just a historical source. Attention turned primarily to the unique material in Chronicles and a new interest developed in the books' message, purpose, setting, theology and historiographical perspective. In general such literary approaches have been undertaken by those who attributed little historical value to the work. In 1930 von Rad published *Das Geschichtsbild des chronistischen Werkes*, in which he emphasized the material unique to Chronicles and explored the historical picture painted by the Chronicler without concern for its historical accuracy.[2] A.C. Welch followed in 1939 with a work which, too, turned away from the issue of historicity and examined the themes and theology of the Chronicler.[3] There he stated:

> It is possible to ignore the demerits of the Chronicler as a historian... and to concentrate attention on what the author had to say, and through the study of what he did say discover, if possible, the purpose he had in writing his book.[4]

Neither von Rad nor Welch considered Chronicles a proper history.[5]

Other works continuing in this trend include: R. North, 'Theology of the Chronicler' (1963); J.M. Myers, 'The Kerygma of the Chronicler' (1966); H. Engler, 'The Attitude of the Chronicler toward the Davidic Monarchy' (1967); R.L. Braun, 'The Significance of 1 Chronicles 22, 28, and 29 for the Structure and Theology of the Work of the Chronicler' (1971); G.E. Schaefer, 'The Significance of Seeking God in the Purpose

---

[1] H.G.M. Williamson, *Israel in the Books of Chronicles* (Cambridge: Cambridge University Press, 1977), pp. 5-70.
[2] Von Rad, *Geschichtsbild*.
[3] Welch, *The Work of the Chronicler*.
[4] *Ibid.*, p. 6.
[5] Von Rad, *Geschichtsbild*, p. 2; Welch, p. 54.

of the Chronicler' (1972); T. Willi, *Die Chronik als Auslegung* (1972); P.R. Ackroyd, 'The Theology of the Chronicler' (1973); W.I. Chang, 'The *Tendenz* of the Chronicler' (1973); S. Japhet, *The Ideology of the Book of Chronicles and its Place in Biblical Thought* (1973); R. Mosis, *Untersuchungen zur Theologie des chronistischen Geschichtswerk* (1973); J.D. Newsome, 'The Chronicler's View of Prophecy' (1973); R. Rigsby, 'The Historiography of Speeches and Prayers in the Books of Chronicles' (1973); H.G.M. Williamson, *Israel in the Book of Chronicles* (1977); W.L. Osborne, 'The Genealogies of I Chronicles 1–9' (1979); Tae-Soo Im, *Das Davidbild in den Chronikbüchern* (1985); M.A. Throntveit, *When Kings Speak: Royal Speech and Royal Prayer in Chronicles* (1987).[1] For the most part these 'literary' and theological studies have been of a literary-historical nature and have addressed such issues as: date and setting, use of sources and/or reliability, and relationship to Ezra–Nehemiah (i.e. Chang, Micheel, Mosis, Newsome, Throntveit, Willi, Williamson). Few have set aside historical concerns and primarily pursued a literary/theological approach (Im, Osborne and Schaefer).

2. Conclusion: The Place of this Book in Chronicles Research
To summarize the above survey: one major trend in Chronicles research, the most dominant one of the last two centuries, has been to approach Chronicles as a historical narrative but to evaluate it as too tendentious to have much value as a historical source. Whereas several scholars in the nineteenth century described the whole work in pejorative terms, most twentieth-century scholars, rather than discarding Chroni-

---

[1] R. North, *JBL* 82 (1963), pp. 369-81; J.M. Myers, *Int* 20 (1966), pp. 259-73; H. Engler (Th.D. dissertation; Union Theological Seminary in Virginia, 1967); R.L. Braun (Th.D. Dissertation; Concordia Seminary, 1971); G.E. Schaefer (Th.D. dissertation; Southern Baptist Theological Seminary, 1972); P.R. Ackroyd, *Lexington Theological Quarterly* 8 (1973), pp. 101-16; W.I. Chang (Ph.D. dissertation; Hartford Seminary Foundation, 1973); S. Japhet ([Hebrew] Ph.D. dissertation; Jerusalem: Hebrew University, 1973), English Abstract, pp. v-xxxviii; W.L. Osborne (Ph.D. dissertation; The Dropsie University, 1979); Tae-Soo Im (Europäische Hochschulschriften, XXIII/263; Frankfurt am Main: Peter Lang, 1985); M.A. Throntveit (SBLDS, 93; Atlanta: Scholars, 1987).

cles as a whole, have seen a need to re-evaluate each individual pericope for any historical data which might be revealed. A second major and more recent trend has been to set aside the question of historical accuracy and to approach Chronicles more as a literary work, to take a new look at the books of Chronicles *per se*, and to examine the role of the author as a creative writer of a theological treatise. Often the goal has still been to answer historical questions, that is, questions regarding authorship, date, history of composition, etc.

This study stands within the trend to approach Chronicles as a literary product without regard for the historical veracity of its material. However, it differs from the majority of previous literary studies. The main questions brought to Chronicles in this study are not literary-historical questions.[1] The goal is not to attach a date to the text, to identify the author, or to examine the issues of unity. Also this study differs from previous ones in bringing to the text a particular kind of literary approach, a rhetorical analysis (the nature of which will be clarified below) which will be applied to derive a sweeping view of the whole of Chronicles.[2]

C. *Methodological Concerns*

1. *The Meaning of 'Rhetoric'*
The title of this book immediately raises the issue of what is meant by 'rhetoric'. Perhaps some think of rhetoric in neutral terms as skillful and artistic speech. Others, who are familiar with the plethora of 'rhetorical' analyses of biblical texts that have been carried out in recent years, will tend to identify it

---

[1] Perhaps a caveat is needed at this point. Since a rhetorical analysis is concerned with the intention of a speaker/author to communicate to the intended audience, one still might broadly categorize this study as having historical concerns. These concerns, however, differ greatly from the typical goals of biblical literary criticism.

[2] As far as this writer knows, there has only been one general analysis of the whole of Chronicles that was expressly 'literary', and that brief article brings no new perspective to the work other than what can be found in most major introductions to the books of Chronicles. See S. Talmon, '1 and 2 Chronicles', *The Literary Guide to the Bible* (ed. R. Alter and F. Kermode; Cambridge, MA: Belknap Press of Harvard University, 1987).

with a 'close reading' of a text. For many the term will have the pejorative connotation of excessively flowery speech, which contains much fluff and little content. For purposes of this study, the first and second concepts are inadequate and the third totally misleading. 'Rhetoric' will be employed in this work in its classical sense, particularly as defined by Aristotle, to denote the art of *persuasive* communication.[1] Given such a broad definition one will realize that much of our experience of verbal communication, written or oral, is rhetorical in nature. We want our audience at least to be persuaded to accept what we are saying as true or valid, and often we want them to act upon it. As Aristotle said, 'The use of persuasive speech is to lead to decisions. (When we know a thing and have decided about it, there is no further use in speaking about it.)'[2] George Kennedy has aptly described how a rhetorical intent pervades most of our communication:

> Rhetoric is a form of communication. The author of a commu- nication has some kind of purpose, and rhetoric certainly includes the ways by which he seeks to accomplish that purpose. The ancient world commonly thought of this purpose as persua- sion, but meant by that something much looser and more inclu- sive than persuasion as understood by a modern social scientist. Purposes cover a whole spectrum from converting hearers to a view opposed to that they previously held, to implanting a convic- tion not otherwise considered, to the deepening of belief in a view already favorably entertained, to a demonstration of the clever- ness of the author, to teaching or exposition. In practice almost every communication is rhetorical in that it uses some device to try to affect the thought, actions, or emotions of an audience, but the degree of rhetoric varies enormously.[3]

---

[1] Aristotle's concept of rhetoric, as stated in his work *Rhetoric*, from which this study draws its method of textual analysis, is further clari- fied in Section D, 'Aristotle's *Rhetoric*'. The translation cited will be *The Basic Works of Aristotle* (ed. R. McKeon; New York: Random House, 1941; *Rhetorica*, trans. W. Rhys Roberts), pp. 1317-1451.

[2] Aristotle, II. 18. 1391b.

[3] G. Kennedy, *Classical Rhetoric and its Christian and Secular Tradi- tion from Ancient to Modern Times* (Chapel Hill: University of North Carolina, 1980), p. 4.

2. *The Rhetorical Nature of Historical Narratives*

We have noted that much of our communication is rhetorical in nature, but it is necessary to take a further step and recognize the rhetorical nature of historical narratives in particular. Contemporary historians and literary critics have demonstrated that historical narratives share in the creative subjective side of story telling.[1] This is to say that 'history', conceived of and communicated in the form of narrative, communicates 'meaning' in the manner that all stories do.

For example, Hayden White, whose work has made a substantial impact on the perspective of this study, defines a historical work as 'a verbal structure in the form of a narrative prose discourse that purports to be a model, or icon, of past structures and processes in the interest of *explaining what they were by representing* them'.[2] He has identified three surface-structural levels through which every historical narrative attributes 'meaning' to the historical field it seeks to represent simply because the writer has perceived and presented the historical field in a narrative/story form:

1. One's narrative 'explains' on the level of emplotment, or story-line, the kind of story in which the participants are involved (i.e. a Romance, Tragedy, Comedy or Satire), because one has conceived a 'course' of history.
2. The narrative 'explains' principles, or 'laws', of combination and coherence which operate in the narrative world (i.e. mechanistic, cause-effect laws versus principles of a

---

[1] P. Hernadi, 'Clio's Cousins: Historiography as Translation, Fiction, and Criticism', *New Literary History* 7 (1976), pp. 245-57; L.O. Mink, 'History and Fiction as Modes of Comprehending', *New Literary Inquiry* 1 (1969/70), pp. 541-58; P. Ricoeur, 'The Narrative Function', *Semeia* 13 (1978), pp. 177-202; R. Scholes and R. Kellogg, *The Nature of Narrative* (Oxford: Oxford University Press, 1966); H. White, *Metahistory* (Baltimore: Johns Hopkins University, 1973); *idem*, 'The Value of Narrativity in the Representation of Reality', *Critical Inquiry* 7 (1980), pp. 5-27; *idem*, 'Rhetoric and History', *Theories of History* (ed. H. White and F.E. Manuel; Los Angeles: University of California, 1978), pp. 3-24.

[2] White, *Metahistory*, p. 2.

synthetic process), because one has conceived relationships among elements of the historical field.[1]

3. And, simply because the narrative tells a kind of story (1)
   in which the various elements have some kind of formal
   coherence (2), by implication the narrative will also
   'explain' an ideology for relevant behavior in that narrative world (i.e. Anarchism, Conservatism, Radicalism or
   Liberalism).[2]

According to this perspective, a historical narrative is no more
than a verbal representation of the historical field as it has
been perceived by those who bring to the task their own individually and culturally shaped models of conceiving reality
and their ideology for action within that reality. To conceive of
something as an 'event' by arbitrarily placing temporal

---

[1] White notes that this means of explaining is the same thing physical
scientists do when they conceive 'laws' of nature. A difference between
historians and scientists is that scientists have reached a greater
degree of agreement as to the form of a scientific explanation, whereas
among historians no such agreement exists (*Metahistory*, pp. 12-13).

[2] Regarding this third level of meaning, White explains further that
one's conception/perception of the past reveals a commitment to a form
of knowledge which then applies to the present by analogy:

> ... the very claim to have discerned some kind of formal coherence in
> the historical record brings with it theories of the nature of the histori-
> cal world and of historical knowledge itself which have ideological
> implications for attempts to understand 'the present', however this
> 'present' is defined. To put it another way, the very claim to have dis-
> tinguished a past from a present world of social thought and praxis,
> and to have determined the formal coherence of the past world,
> *implies* a conception of the form that knowledge of the present world
> also must take insofar as it is *continuous* with that past world. Com-
> mitment to a particular *form* of knowledge predetermines the *kinds* of
> generalizations one can make about the present world ... (*Meta-
> history*, p. 21).

These three levels of meaning are discussed in *Metahistory* (pp. 1-29).
White also finds a fourth level below the surface of the historical narrative, a 'metaphysical' level at which a historian finds meaning.
Prior to explaining and representing the historical field, a historian
must perceive it as a domain with discernible figures bearing certain
kinds of relationships among them. This act of perceiving or
'prefiguring' is essentially a poetic act, because it is precognitive and
precritical. This act establishes the structures subsequently imagined
in the verbal body of the historian's account (*Metahistory*, pp. 30-32).

parameters in a continuum of the historical field, to focus on a particular subject matter, to select particular events to record, and to arrange those events into an ordered narrative are actions which derive from and manifest one's mode of perception, one's conceptions about the world and how it operates, and one's ideological principles about how one should or should not operate within such a world.

In answering the question, 'Why do stories bear repeating?', Louis Mink has also provided a reason why historians write histories:

> ... because they aim at producing and strengthening the act of understanding in which actions and events, although represented as occurring in the order of time, can be surveyed as it were in a single glance as bound together in an order of significance, a representation of the *totum simul* which we can never more than partially achieve.[1]

Historical narratives are representational depictions of the world composed for the purpose of conveying 'meaning' to one's audience. The historian wishes to persuade the audience to accept her or his story as true—that means to accept it with its inherent presuppositions, world-view and ideology. Each historical narrative informs its audience and confronts it with the need to make a variety of decisions: to judge a past act, to assess praise or blame, to accept certain laws of coherence among events, to believe there is a certain course to history, etc. And, the degree to which the audience does accept the story as 'true' depends on how convincing the historian was. The real source of appeal of a historical work, that which makes it acceptably 'realistic' or 'objective' to one's readers, is, according to White, rhetorical in nature.[2] Therefore, every historical narrative, including the books of Chronicles, functions rhetorically and can be examined in terms of its persuasive artistry.

3. *The Nature and Goal of a Rhetorical Analysis*
A rhetorical-critical study of a literary unit is interested in the literary artistry of the author/editor towards persuasive ends.

---

[1] Mink, p. 554.
[2] White, 'Rhetoric and History', p. 3.

Every rhetorical act involves a speaker/composer, an audience and a verbal product. Some exigency arises which motivates the rhetor to speak. The rhetor within that situation begins the rhetorical process with a message to communicate and with a perceived audience to receive the communication. He or she then must arrive at a strategy of communication, which hopefully will motivate that audience to receive and act on the message. This strategy may be arrived at deliberately or even rather unconsciously. Involved in this strategy are the decisions one makes about the types of arguments, modes of persuasion, kinds of material, arrangement of material and choice of words.

A 'rhetorical analysis' refers then to the discovery of the artistic means of persuasion employed in the communication through an analysis of the finished work. A rhetorical analysis must work backwards from the finished product and re-create certain constituents. It attempts to identify those 'elements' which would have had a persuasive appeal to the audience and to re-create the strategy employed by the author. As such, a rhetorical analysis, although proceeding by a disciplined method, is still a subjective and creative literary task.

The rhetorical-critical approach of this study to the books of Chronicles will build on many of the observations made by previous critical studies of Chronicles; however, its perspective and objectives differ. It is the objective of this approach to arrive at a clearer picture of the Chronicler's purpose (what he wanted the audience to believe/do) and how he attempted to effect this purpose through his particular rhetorical strategy. A rhetorical approach offers something different from other critical approaches. George Kennedy has summed up that difference in this manner:

> For some readers of the Bible rhetorical criticism may have an appeal lacking to other modern critical approaches, in that it comes closer to explaining what they want explained in the text: not its sources, but its power. Rhetoric cannot describe the historical Jesus or identify Matthew or John; they are probably irretrievably lost to scholarship. But it does study a verbal reality, our text of the Bible, rather than the oral sources standing behind that text, the hypothetical stages of its composition, or the impersonal working of social forces, and at its best it can reveal

the power of these texts as unitary messages. The Bible speaks through ethos, logos and pathos,[1] and to understand these is the concern of rhetorical analysis.[2]

4. *The Designation of Chronicles as a Rhetorical Unit*
Another concern which needs to be clarified is the designation of Chronicles as a rhetorical unit. Although there may be more than one source or hand behind the present text of Chronicles, this study will not focus on issues relating to the history of the composition of Chronicles. The present study will deal with the text in its Massoretic form, since that is the material directly available, rather than with hypothetical reconstructions. Indeed, the aim of a rhetorical analysis may be stated to be to examine a work synchronically.

> Rhetorical criticism takes the text as we have it, whether the work of a single author or the product of editing, and looks at it from the point of view of the author's or editor's intent, the unified results, and how it would be perceived by an audience of near contemporaries.[3]

The original intention and setting of sources used in a work are not the point of focus. Such sources have become transformed according to their role in the final work.[4] Therefore, the focus is on the intention of the final composer. And, one must conclude that the present form of the work expresses the

[1] 'Ethos', 'logos' and 'pathos' are rhetorical terms which refer to modes of persuasion. They are further clarified in Section D, 'Aristotle's *Rhetoric*', and in the subsequent chapters which analyze each mode of persuasion.
[2] G. Kennedy, *New Testament Interpretation through Rhetorical Criticism* (Chapel Hill: University of North Carolina, 1984), pp. 158-59.
[3] *Ibid.*, p. 4.
[4] N.R. Petersen ('Literary Criticism in Biblical Studies', *Orientation by Disorientation* [ed. R.A. Spencer; Pittsburgh: Pickwick, 1980], p. 36) has defended the priority of examining the whole of a text before its parts:

> The authors are, to whatever degree, responsible for the whole. Therefore, to start with the whole makes sense, more sense than starting with the parts that may have no authorially intentional function in the whole but be in it only because they were in the author's sources.

intent of the final major composer/editor.[1] This final composer
will be referred to as the 'Chronicler'. Since Chronicles is
found in the Hebrew Bible as a complete work, separate from
Ezra–Nehemiah, it will be analyzed in its own right.[2]

5. *Reading Chronicles with regard to Samuel–Kings*

Some students of Chronicles have come either to the conclusion that Chronicles is an interpretation of the Deuteronomistic History[3] or at least parts of it are a 'midrashic' exegesis
of that history.[4] If one is working with the conclusion that
Samuel–Kings was the primary source of the Chronicler, the
exploration of the Chronicler's use of and transformation of
this material is unquestionably a legitimate scholarly pursuit.
However, reading Chronicles as an interpretation of Samuel–
Kings would appear to be contrary to the type of reading
intended by the Chronicler. Chronicles makes no claim to be
an interpretation of or commentary on Samuel–Kings or any
other historical record. It presents itself as a valid historical
narrative in its own right. To assume that the intended reading of Chronicles was to be a detailed synoptic-comparative
reading is to foist the methods and concerns of modern scholarship on the ancient audience.[5] Further, if the Chronicler,
knowing Samuel–Kings or other sources, chose to include
certain material and reject other, he did so according to his
rhetorical strategy in order to better demonstrate his argument. To fail to read Chronicles as an independent work is to
miss the rhetorical nature and intent of the work.

At the same time, it appears that the Chronicler's intended
audience was not expected to be unaware of the material
found in Samuel–Kings. The Chronicler's citation of sources

[1] By referring to the final 'major' composer we are allowing for later,
minor changes such as extending genealogies and lists and moderniz-
ing place names.
[2] Those who support the thesis of the unity of Chronicles with Ezra–
Nehemiah may wish to carry the analysis further to see if the rhetorical strategy is consistent throughout.
[3] Most recently, Willi (*Die Chronik als Auslegung*) has argued that
Chronicles should be read as an interpretation of Samuel–Kings.
[4] Barnes, 'The Midrashic Element in Chronicles'.
[5] So, too, observes Michael Fishbane, *Biblical Interpretation in
Ancient Israel* (Oxford: Clarendon, 1985), pp. 381-82.

throughout his work indicates that he assumed his audience accepted the existence of other written 'historical' material.[1] Also, the Chronicler's narrative makes allusions to events not contained in his story, but found in Samuel–Kings (e.g. 1 Chron. 11.3 refers to how David became king according to the word of Samuel, which is found in 1 Sam. 16; and 2 Chron. 10.15 refers to the fulfillment of the prophecy of Ahijah, which is recorded at 1 Kgs 11.29-39).[2] Such allusions demand the conclusion that the audience was expected to know at least some of the traditions found in Samuel–Kings whether or not they knew that particular work.

Therefore, one of our working assumptions will be that the Chronicler did not expect his audience to make a detailed, synoptic comparison of his work to some other work, but he did expect them to have a general familiarity with the traditional material he intended to present. This situation presented the Chronicler with the rhetorical problem of how to re-present traditional material in a manner that would be convincing to his audience.[3]

6. *The Utilization of Aristotle's* Rhetoric

This study employs a method of rhetorical analysis drawn primarily from Aristotle's *Rhetoric*. The decision to be depen-

[1] Even if the Chronicler's citations were fabricated, as some scholars have assumed, he still presumably capitalized on the audience's belief in the existence of and authority of such written records.

[2] See also B.S. Childs, *Introduction to the Old Testament as Scripture* (Philadelphia: Fortress, 1979), pp. 646-47, and P.R. Ackroyd, 'The Chronicler as Exegete', *JSOT* 2 (1977), p. 21.

[3] In the above section, and throughout this work, certain general assumptions are made about the knowledge of and expectations of the Chronicler's intended audience. The attempt to recreate, very broadly, the intended audience and to imagine its reactions to the Chronicler and to his account, as well as the identification of the author of the work with the narrator within the work, are methodological devices which overlap with some of the approaches of 'reader-response criticism'. (See W.G. Gibson, 'Authors, Speakers, Readers and Mock Readers', and G. Prince, 'Introduction to the Study of the Narratee', both in *Reader-Response Criticism* [ed. J.P. Tompkins; Baltimore: Johns Hopkins University, 1980], pp. 1-6 and 7-25, respectively.) It is not the concern of this study, however, to identify more precisely the actual historical setting of the audience of the Chronicler.

dent specifically on Aristotle is grounded in the fact that his work is one of the earliest and most influential descriptive works on rhetoric.[1] Concerning Aristotle's work, Kennedy states, 'If one looks back over the first hundred and fifty years of rhetorical theory, Aristotle's *Rhetoric* seems to tower above all the remains... Its influence has been enormous and still continues.'[2]

But, what justifies the application of a classical Greek work on rhetoric to an ancient Israelite historical narrative? Would not Israelite rhetoric be colored by its own cultural features and be quite different from Greek rhetoric? In terms of style, to some degree, the answer would be yes. Stylistic features do vary from culture to culture. But the basic devices of invention, the planning of arguments, are less dependent on cultural differences than are features of style.[3] In his opening statement on rhetoric Aristotle observed:

> Rhetoric is the counterpart of Dialectic. Both alike are concerned with such things as come, more or less, within the general ken of all men and belong to no definite science. Accordingly all men make use, more or less, of both; for to a certain extent all men attempt to discuss statements and to maintain them, to defend themselves and to attack others. Ordinary people do this either at random or through practice and from acquired habit. Both ways being possible, the subject can plainly be handled systematically, for it is possible to inquire the reason why some speakers succeed through practice and others spontaneously; and every one will at once agree that such an inquiry is the function of an art.[4]

Two key points in this introductory statement should be noted. First, all people engage in the activity of rhetoric. It is a uni-

---

[1] Two complete handbooks from the second half of the fourth century BCE have been preserved: *Rhetorica ad Alexandrum* and Aristotle's *Rhetoric*. Although earlier works are referred to, no works prior to Aristotle have survived. *Rhetorica ad Alexandrum*, preserved in the corpus of Aristotle, is probably a typical product of early sophistic rhetoric of which Aristotle disapproved (G. Kennedy, *The Art of Persuasion in Greece* [Princeton: Princeton University Press, 1963], pp. 81, 114-15).

[2] *Ibid.*, p. 123.

[3] Kennedy, *New Testament Interpretation*, p. 8.

[4] Aristotle, I. 1. 1354a.

versal phenomenon of human communication. Aristotle's *Rhetoric* was not written as a prescriptive work, although it was used for training rhetors. Neither did he intend it merely to be descriptive of Greek rhetoric. He sought to describe the universal characteristics of persuasion.[1] As such, the system set forth in the *Rhetoric* may be applied to any literary composition with persuasive ends. Secondly, rhetoric is an art, not a science. That is to say, as an art it does not theorize about logical necessities as a science does. Rather, it is akin to dialectic, which is the art of reasoning about probabilities.[2] And as an art rhetoric is open to systematic inquiry in an attempt to understand how one persuades successfully.[3]

One reservation must be expressed before applying Aristotle's systematic exploration of rhetoric to the books of Chronicles. Aristotle described the art of rhetoric with speech forms in mind as the mode of communication, not historical narratives. However, as has been remarked above, many forms of communication serve rhetorical purposes, including historical narratives. And, many of Aristotle's observations apply to narratives as well as to speeches.[4] Therefore, this writer has sought to include observations of Aristotle which lend themselves also to narrative analysis, and to exclude those which apply only to speeches.

D. *Aristotle's 'Rhetoric'*

1. *Introduction*
The *Rhetoric* consists of three books, which probably represent Aristotle's thought on this subject during his period of teaching in Athens, 335–323 BCE.[5] It was a draft of his theories to be used in his teaching and was not intended for publication. The

---

[1] Kennedy, *New Testament Interpretation*, pp. 10-11; and C.S. Baldwin, *Ancient Rhetoric and Poetic* (New York: Macmillan, 1924), p. 8.
[2] Kennedy, *Classical Rhetoric*, pp. 62-63.
[3] See W. Grimaldi, *Aristotle, Rhetoric I: A Commentary* (Bronx, NY: Fordham University, 1980), pp. 4-5, for a discussion of the concept of *techné*, 'art'.
[4] For an example of categories of classical rhetoric applied to other biblical narratives, see Kennedy, *New Testament Interpretation*.
[5] Kennedy, *Classical Rhetoric*, p. 61.

work is not fully schematized or refined but shows evidence of additions, elaborations and development of thought. For this reason some points in it remain obscure.[1] Very basically, the first two books deal with the invention of arguments and the third with the style and arrangement of the speech material.

In the culture of Aristotle, being a skilled orator was a great asset, if not a necessity. Citizens were expected to defend themselves in court cases, since there were no professional lawyers. Aristotle stated four reasons why rhetoric was useful: (1) One needed to be able to present the truth well, in order for the truth to prevail in the decision of judges. (2) Persuasion can produce conviction in an audience which otherwise would be unable to receive and comprehend technical instruction. (3) Persuasive speech should be employed on both sides of a question in order to make sure the facts are seen clearly. (4) One ought to be able to defend oneself not just with one's limbs, but with speech and reason, particularly since rational speech is distinctive to human beings.[2]

According to Aristotle, 'Rhetoric may be defined as the faculty of observing in any given case the available means of persuasion'.[3] It is the theoretical activity of perceiving or discovering the knowledge of, for example, the words, arguments, topics, arrangement and style which make up a speech and render it persuasive.

2. The Parts of Rhetoric
Aristotle stated:

> In making a speech one must study three points: first, the means of producing persuasion; second, the style, or language, to be used; third, the proper arrangement of the various parts of the speech...

> Our next subject will be the style of expression. For it is not enough to know *what* we ought to say; we must also say it *as* we ought; much help is thus afforded towards producing the right

[1] *Ibid.* L. Arnhart finds a more unified organization than do many scholars, on the basis of his perception that Aristotle's discussion moves from the particular to the general (*Aristotle on Political Reasoning* [DeKalb: Northern Illinois University, 1981], pp. 51-53).
[2] Aristotle, I. 1. 1355a.
[3] *Ibid.*, I. 2. 1355b.

impression of a speech. The first question to receive attention was naturally the one that comes first naturally—how persuasion can be produced from the facts themselves. The second is how to set these facts out in language. A third would be the proper method of delivery; this is a thing that affects the success of a speech greatly; but hitherto the subject has been neglected.[1]

Although Aristotle mentions only three points, this description of the aspects of rhetoric appears to have been the basis of the standard five-part division of rhetoric that occurs in later treatises on rhetoric: invention, arrangement, style, memory and delivery.[2] 'Invention' refers to the development of strategy regarding the means of producing persuasion. 'Arrangement' refers to the order of the primary parts of the speech. By 'style' is meant the appropriate use of language. 'Memory', the only aspect which Aristotle did not discuss, refers to the process of committing speeches to memory. And, 'delivery', on which Aristotle included some observations, treats the art of oral presentation.

For the purpose of this book a discussion of the aspects of memory and delivery would be irrelevant, since a written product is being analyzed. Regarding 'style', Aristotle taught that the language must be clear, must be correct in terms of grammar, must be appropriate in its use of adornment or figures, and should have a sense of rhythm.[3] Observations of this nature will be general and incidental, since this analysis of Chronicles is intended to present a panoramic picture of the whole and not to give a detailed view of small, individual units.

Regarding the arrangement of the primary parts, Aristotle had only a few comments. He allowed that a speech could have several parts, including an introduction, a comparison of conflicting arguments, a recapitulation, an accusation, a defence and an epilogue. His main point, though, was to note that the only essential parts were a statement of the case and the argument that sought to prove the statement.[4] However, the importance of arrangement from another perspective is not to be overlooked. The structure of a narrative establishes

[1] *Ibid.*, III. 1. 1403b, pp. 15-20.
[2] Kennedy, *Classical Rhetoric*, pp. 77-78.
[3] *Ibid.*, pp. 78-79.
[4] Aristotle, III. 13.

Forms of Proof in Aristotle's *Rhetoric*

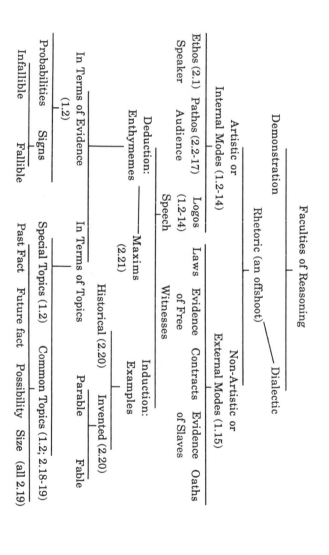

a story-line with its resultant 'meaning' and facilitates the demonstration of the rhetor's arguments. Departing somewhat from Aristotle's *Rhetoric*, this study will also incorporate some observations from the perspective of 'poetics' regarding the structure of the Chronicler's narrative (Chapter 2). Of first importance, though, is 'invention', the act of discovering the 'material' of the speech, that is, the arguments and their topics, and the modes of persuasion. It is upon this aspect of rhetoric that this study will focus, with the greatest emphasis given to the three persuasive appeals (Chapters 3, 4 and 5).

In the following synopsis of the main features of *Rhetoric*, which we want to incorporate in our analysis of Chronicles, the chart opposite, taken from Kennedy's *Classical Rhetoric*, should provide some guidance.[1]

3. *Modes of Persuasion*

Persuasion is achieved in part through the *pisteis*. The *pisteis* are variously rendered 'proofs', 'appeals', and 'modes of persuasion'. Perhaps with Grimaldi and Arnhart, who seem to define them with Aristotle's system of causality in mind, they should be viewed as the *material* sources of persuasion.[2] There are two kinds of *pisteis*, artistic or internal ones and nonartistic or external ones:

> Of the modes of persuasion some belong strictly to the art of rhetoric and some do not. By the latter I mean such things as are not supplied by the speaker but are there at the outset—witnesses, evidence given under torture, written contracts, and so on. By the former I mean such as we can ourselves construct by means of the principles of rhetoric. The one kind has merely to be used, the other has to be invented.[3]

Aristotle did not focus on the external proofs, for these are not created by the rhetor; they in themselves do not represent the artistic side of rhetoric. However, it is important to observe

---

[1] Kennedy, *Classical Rhetoric*, p. 69.
[2] Aristotle's four causes are: the material, the formal, the efficient and the final. Grimaldi and Arnhart discriminate between material means of effecting persuasion through the artistic *pisteis* and the formal process through the enthymeme and example (Grimaldi, p. 352; Arnhart, pp. 35-38).
[3] Aristotle, I. 2. 1356a.

how the external proofs fit in with the strategy of the rhetor.
Why were certain ones selected over others? Where and how
did the rhetor use external proofs? What kinds of external
proofs were utilized? How would the audience have received
them? Those proofs which Aristotle mentioned belong primarily to speeches concerned with legal decisions. Others are
possible. George Kennedy found that in the New Testament
three kinds of external proof were common: quotations of the
Old Testament, miracles and naming witnesses.[1] An analysis
of Chronicles will need to identify the external witnesses used
in the work and their strategic importance.

The artistic modes or proofs, on which Aristotle focused,
correspond to the three foci of the speech-act: the speaker, the
audience and the speech.

> Of the modes of persuasion furnished by the spoken word there
> are three kinds. The first kind depends on the personal charac-
> ter [*ethos*] of the speaker; the second on putting the audience
> into a certain frame of mind [*pathos*]; the third on the proof, or
> apparent proof provided by the words of the speech itself [*logos*].
> Persuasion is achieved by the speaker's personal character
> [*ethos*] when the speech is so spoken as to make us think him
> credible... Secondly, persuasion may come through the hear-
> ers, when the speech stirs their emotions [*pathos*]... Thirdly,
> when persuasion is effected through the speech [*logos*] itself
> when we have proved a truth or an apparent truth by means of
> the persuasive arguments suitable to the case in question.
>   There are, then, these three means of effecting persuasion.
> The man who is to be in command of them must, it is clear, be
> able (1) to reason logically [*logos*], (2) to understand human
> character [*ethos*] and goodness in their various forms and (3) to
> understand the emotions [*pathos*]...[2]

In the above translation, an English transliteration of the key
terms, which have come to be used to identify the three artistic
pisteis described by Aristotle, have been included within
brackets. These are: 'ethos', the means of appeal based on the
character of the speaker as it comes through the speech to the
audience; 'pathos', the means of appeal as the speech moves
the audience's emotions; and 'logos', the speech itself as it

---

[1] Kennedy, *New Testament Interpretation*, p. 14.
[2] Aristotle, I. 2. 1356a.

makes an appeal on the level of logical reasoning. Our analysis of Chronicles will observe how these means of appeal effect the persuasive quality of the book.

4. *Types of Rhetorical Speech*

Aristotle recognized that the degree to which one used each of these three means of persuasion depended on the purpose of the speech. Until his time the various kinds of oratory had not been classified into genres. To this end Aristotle originated a classification of three genres of speech which has become a permanent feature of rhetorical theory: (1) deliberative or political, (2) legal or forensic and (3) epideictic or ceremonial.[1]

> Rhetoric falls into three divisions, determined by the three classes of listeners to speeches. For of the three elements in speech-making—speaker, subject and person addressed—it is the last one, the hearer, that determines the speech's end and object. The hearer must be either a judge, with a decision to make about things past or future, or an observer. A member of the assembly decides about future events, a juryman about past events: while those who merely decide on the orator's skill are observers. From this it follows that there are three divisions of oratory—(1) political, (2) forensic and (3) the ceremonial oratory of display.
>
> Political speaking urges us either to do or not to do something: one of these two courses is always taken by private counsellors, as well as by men who address public assemblies. Forensic speaking either attacks or defends somebody: one or other of these two things must always be done by the parties in a case. The ceremonial oratory of display either praises or censures somebody. These three kinds of rhetoric refer to three different kinds of time. The political orator is concerned with the future: it is about things to be done hereafter that he advises, for or against. The party in a case at law is concerned with the past; one man accuses the other, and the other defends himself, with reference to things already done. The ceremonial oratory is, properly speaking, concerned with the present, since all men praise or blame in view of the state of things existing at the time, though they often find it useful also to recall the past and to make guesses at the future.[2]

---

[1] Kennedy, *Classical Rhetoric*, p. 72.
[2] Aristotle, I. 3. 1358a-1358b.

Each of these kinds of rhetoric has a distinct end in view. Political rhetoric aims at establishing the expediency or harmfulness of a proposed course of action. Forensic speech aims at establishing the justice or injustice of an action that has taken place. Ceremonial oratory aims at establishing that someone is either worthy of honor or of the reverse.[1] Further observation will be made about the type of rhetoric employed in Chronicles in the final section of Chapter 2 after an analysis of how the work is structured to communicate the Chronicler's message.

[1] Aristotle, I. 3. 1358b.

Chapter 2

PURPOSE, STRUCTURE AND TYPE OF RHETORIC

A. *Introduction*

The goals of this chapter are, first, to set forth a major purpose of the composition of Chronicles, secondly, to examine how the parts of this work are structured to communicate its purpose persuasively, and, lastly, to identify the rhetorical category Chronicles most resembles. To present a conclusion regarding a purpose of Chronicles and then to demonstrate a structure based on the assumption of this purpose involves a methodology circular in nature. It is, however, circular by necessity. One cannot describe the structure and arrangement of a narrative without already having reached some conclusion, however tentative, about the nature of the story being told and its emplotment or story-line. This is to say that one cannot make an analysis of the parts of a narrative without first having a comprehension of the whole. Any claim to set forth some pristine, inductive examination of the structure of a text in order to 'discover' its 'meaning' would be misleading. Rather, a prior level of comprehension results in a hypothesis regarding the purpose and message of the text, and this hypothesis is then employed to explain/understand the text's structure. The results of this effort should be evaluated on the basis of whether or not the hypothesis regarding a purpose and the resulting observations regarding the structure produce a satisfactory model for an understanding of the narrative.

B. *A Purpose of the Chronicler*

Reference has been made initially to setting forth *a* major purpose of the Chronicler rather than *the* purpose, for several reasons. Even when a historical narrative is created totally by only one hand, its composer quite naturally might have more than one thought or argument to communicate. Then, too, the composer might communicate a message entirely other than that which was intended. Every reader will approach a text with different paradigms for 'finding' meaning, and will, therefore, discover different purposes behind a text. This study brings to the text paradigms for finding meaning which have been adopted from the approaches of Hayden White and Aristotle.[1] The level at which this writer is seeking to identify a purpose is on the surface structure of the narrative, with particular emphasis on the nature of the emplotment. Therefore, the purpose which this writer identifies, though it is believed to be a major intention of the Chronicler, must be recognized as one of many that can be perceived or conceived.

Scholars of the books of Chronicles have arrived at a great number of conclusions regarding the purpose/s of the book. There is no consensus opinion. Purposes proposed have included: to present a theory of the return of 'all Israel' from exile (Torrey[2]), to defend post-exilic cultic institutions (Curtis and Madsen, Noth, Myers[3]), to write a history of the Davidic dynasty in terms of its religious and cultic accomplishments (Freedman[4]), to defend the realization of the theocracy in the new community of Israel against the claims of the Samaritans (Pfeiffer, Noth, Rudolph[5]), to write a history of Judah and its institutions (Driver[6]), to teach religious values through history (Keil, Welch, Mosis[7]), to strive to maintain religious orthodoxy

---

[1] See Chapter 1, section C, 'Methodological Concerns'.

[2] C.C. Torrey, *The Chronicler's History of Israel* (New Haven: Yale University, 1954), pp. xxiv-xxv.

[3] Curtis and Madsen, p. 9; Noth, *Studien*, p. 174; Myers, *1 Chronicles*, pp. xxx-lx.

[4] Freedman, p. 437.

[5] R.H. Pfeiffer, *An Introduction to the Old Testament* (2nd edn; New York: Harper & Brothers, 1948), pp. 802, 806; Noth, *Studien*, p. 166; Rudolph, *Chronikbücher*, pp. viii-ix.

[6] S.R. Driver, *An Introduction to the Literature of the Old Testament* (9th edn; Edinburgh: T. & T. Clark, 1913), p. 517.

[7] C.F. Keil and F. Delitzsch, *Biblical Commentary on the Old Testament* (25 vols.; Clark's Foreign Theological Library, 4th ser.; Edinburgh: T. & T. Clark, 1878; reprint edn; Grand Rapids: Eerdmans,

(Myers[1]), and to interpret to the restored community the history of Israel as an eternal covenant between God and David, a covenant which demanded obedience to the law (Childs[2]).

At first glance many of the proposals might seem quite disparate. Yet in reality there are some common observations that several of them share. First, descriptions of the Chronicler's motivation as the intention 'to write a history' do not necessarily conflict with such descriptions as 'to demonstrate something by historical narrative'. If one recognizes that writing a historical narrative is a creative and subjective task, then one can accept that the Chronicler's purpose was not to write an unachievable 'objective' history, but 'to teach' or 'to defend' through a historical narrative. The above mentioned positions basically agree that the Chronicler wanted to persuade his audience about something by means of the narrative. Second, most of these proposals hold in common the observation that the Chronicler stressed the importance of the institutions of the Davidic monarchy and the Jerusalem cultus. Third, this writer believes that the above scholars would have also recognized a common feature regarding the Chronicler's world view: the Israelite God, Yahweh, was active in the course of history, effecting blessing and punishment, particularly in regard to matters involving the Davidic dynasty and the temple cultus.[3]

The thesis which I believe best incorporates the above points of 'agreement' has been set forth by G.E. Schaefer in his dissertation, 'The Significance of Seeking God in the Purpose of the Chronicler':

1978), vol. 7: *The Books of Chronicles* by C.F. Keil, p. 19; Welch, pp. 54, 123; Mosis, p. 223.

[1] Myers, *1 Chronicles*, pp. xxx-xl.

[2] Childs, p. 644.

[3] Raymond B. Dillard ('Reward and Punishment in Chronicles: The Theology of Immediate Retribution', *WTJ* 46 [1984], pp. 164-65) has noted that although there has been much debate through the history of research on Chronicles over the author's theology, date and purpose, on one theme there is a near consensus: the recognition that the Chronicler holds a theology of immediate retribution of punishment for sin and of blessing for righteousness; and the recognition that this perspective plays a dominant role in shaping the Chronicler's composition.

The primary aim of the Chronicler was to demonstrate from history that a faithful adherence to the 'God of the fathers' results in happiness and blessing and that forsaking the LORD will lead the nation and individual to ruin and curse. His high-lighting of the reigns of David and Solomon was to demonstrate that one is to seek the LORD through the temple cultus that was established in Jerusalem by them and honored by subsequent kings. The Chronicler's emphasis on 'seeking the LORD' is to be understood as an invitation extended to the people to experience life on its highest plane. His desire was to see the theocracy realized in Israel, with the people giving themselves completely to the LORD and looking to him to meet all their needs.[1]

'Seeking the LORD' meant a total response of the worshiper to God. One turned to, prayed to, inquired of, trusted, praised and worshiped Yahweh and no other god. Most importantly, one did so through the proper cultic means in the proper cultic place. The opposite of seeking was not so much the commission of a sinful action, but an unfaithfulness demonstrated by failing to turn to Yahweh and by neglecting the temple cultus.[2] The resultant blessing or cursing, although usually centered on the king, impacted the well-being of the whole nation. Blessing took a variety of forms: victory in battle, rest from one's enemies, united support of the people, prosperity, wisdom, healing, the ability to execute building projects or to increase one's army and fortifications. Cursing or retribution took the opposite forms: military defeat, illness or death, rebellion of the people, etc.[3]

Schaefer substantiated his thesis by focusing on the material unique to Chronicles and by demonstrating that the Chronicler set forth the axiom of 'seeking Yahweh' in a variety of literary forms: poetry, regnal formulae, prophetic speeches, sermons, prayers and straight narrative. He not only examined the key phrase, 'to seek Yahweh' (expressed with either דרש or בקש), but also explored the range of vocabulary

---

[1] Schaefer, pp. 17-18.
[2] Schaefer, Chapter 3.
[3] Rudolph, *Chronikbücher*, pp. xviii-xx; Braun, pp. 169-81, 204; Dillard, 'Reward and Punishment', pp. 165-70; Welten. See also the chart of these indications of blessing and cursing at the end of this chapter.

employed by the Chronicler to support this concept, including terms for: forsaking God, turning/repenting, humbling oneself, trusting, worshiping, praising, praying. Schaefer's thesis, then, with some modification and amplification, has been adopted as the basis for my understanding of the purpose of the Chronicler. To state this thesis in other words, a major intention of the Chronicler was to persuade his audience by the example of Israel's (Judah's) history that they should 'seek Yahweh' and uphold the proper temple cultus in order to receive blessing. Inherent in this purpose is a defense of cultic and political institutions as well as an explanation of the exile.

C. *Structure*

1. *Introduction*
Given the above premise regarding the Chronicler's purpose, the next step is to examine how Chronicles has been structured to communicate this purpose. Our analysis of Chronicles will go beyond a simple identification of speech parts and will turn towards a more literary analysis of the structure of the narration. Still, it is helpful to start with some observations by Aristotle about the rhetorical understanding of arrangement. According to Aristotle, a speech basically has two main parts, the statement of the case and the argument.[1] Although he recognized that speeches often include two more parts, an introduction and an epilogue, his emphasis on the two basic parts ran contrary to the popular rhetorical theories of his day which required that a speech have many parts.[2] According to these popular theories, one part was devoted to proof and the other parts to making various emotional appeals. For Aristotle, however, the emotionally oriented appeals of ethos and pathos were integral parts of the presentation of the argument and not to be used to sway the audience apart from the rational argument.[3]

As has been noted, the Chronicler's 'speech', in the form of a historical narrative, does not represent the typical kind of

[1] Aristotle, III. 13. 1414a30-35.
[2] Arnhart, p. 177.
[3] *Ibid.*; Aristotle, I. 1. 1354a12-35.

speech with which Aristotle dealt. Still, it can be viewed as having rhetorical parts. As we shall develop in the following section, the first nine chapters, consisting of lists and genealogies, function as an introduction. An introduction, according to Aristotle, should pave the way to what follows, giving the hearers a foretaste of what is to come and/or clearing away any obstacles regarding the speaker, hearers or subject matter.[1] My belief is that the genealogical section in Chronicles both leads the audience into the subject and thesis of the narrative and disposes the audience to a favorable reception of the speaker.[2] The material following the genealogies, when viewed broadly in terms of function, consists of two major sections. 1 Chronicles 10–2 Chronicles 9, which treats the period from Saul through Solomon, establishes the major paradigm about seeking Yahweh. The remaining chapters, which cover the reigns of the kings of Judah, 2 Chronicles 10–36, present repeated demonstrations of this paradigm in the history of Israel. Generally speaking, these parts function respectively as the introduction, the statement of the case and the demonstration of the case.[3]

[1] Aristotle, III. 14.

[2] This point, regarding the audience's reception of the speaker, is developed in Chapter 4. George Kennedy has observed that the genealogies in Matthew play a similar role. They set the stage for the proposition and serve as external proof establishing the authoritative ethos of Jesus (*New Testament Interpretation*, pp. 102-103).

[3] Throntveit finds three main periods indicated by structural devices: a period of unity under David and Solomon; the Divided Monarchy, from Rehoboam up through part of Hezekiah's reign; and the period of the Re-united Monarchy, from Hezekiah onwards. His support for a distinct period of the Divided Monarchy rests on two structures he finds. The first consists of two 'call-to-return' speeches by Abijah (2 Chron. 13.4-12) and Hezekiah (30.6-9) which bracket this period. Supposedly, these speeches serve the purpose of calling the Northern Kingdom to return to the proper cultic and political institutions. The second consists of a chiastic structure of royal speeches unique to Chronicles which fall within this bracketing. The purpose of this structuring, according to Throntveit, was to communicate to the audience the need for unity (see Throntveit, pp. 113-20). Two problems exist with this thesis. First, to this reader, not all of the elements of the chiasm correspond. The first speech by Abijah contains no explicit call to return as does its counterpart. It is a warning for the North not to attack rather than an invitation to re-unite. Other elements of the

Having identified the main 'parts' of Chronicles, my goal in the following sections is to describe more fully the significance of these parts and to explore further how the arrangement and the structure of the narrative contribute to a persuasive communication of the Chronicler's purpose. Several studies, particularly in recent Chronicles research, have uncovered various rhetorical, structural devices. Scholars have noted the use of *inclusio*, chiasm, typology, repeated motifs and contrasting motifs.[1] Having approached a study of Chronicles for the purpose of writing a homiletical commentary, Leslie Allen discovered that various rhetorical devices served to subdivide Chronicles into short units which could be assimilated easily by an audience. He commented:

> It was hard to avoid an impression that the material had itself been composed on homiletic lines, in order to present a series of self-contained messages in literary form.[2]

What emerges from this study is a sense of the Chronicler's literary and homiletic skills. He indulged in widespread usage of the standard techniques of rhetorical criticism and used them as signals of his kerygmatic intentions. By means of such techniques he presented his material in assimilable portions, high-

chiasm also seem weak. A more significant problem exists, however. Even granting the plausibility that the Chronicler worked some such structure into his narrative, it is unlikely that it would have carried much persuasive impact. It seems safe to presume that a Hebrew audience would be sensitive to literary patterns; but to perceive Throntveit's pattern, they would have to listen/read very selectively. For the audience to make the same observation, they would have to read synoptically and discard parallel speech material, as well as other instances of direct speech by kings and prophets.

1 L.C. Allen, 'Kerygmatic Units in 1 & 2 Chronicles' *JSOT* 41 (1988), pp. 21-36; R.B. Dillard, 'The Chronicler's Solomon', *WTJ* 43 (1980), pp. 299-300, and 'The Literary Structure of the Chronicler's Solomon Narrative', *JSOT* 30 (1984) pp. 85-93; H.G.M. Williamson, '"We are yours, O David": The Setting and Purpose of 1 Chronicles xii 1-23', *Remembering All the Way* (OTS, 21; Leiden: E.J. Brill, 1981), pp. 168-70, and *1 and 2 Chronicles*, e.g. pp. 46-47, 49-50, 96-97. For a thorough form-critical study of structures in Chronicles, see S.J. De Vries, *1 and 2 Chronicles* (The Forms of the Old Testament Literature, 11; Grand Rapids: Eerdmans, 1989).

2 Allen, 'Kerygmatic Units', p. 4.

lighting various themes in order to communicate his distinctive theological and devotional message.[1]

For the most part these earlier studies have concentrated on devices of rhetoric used in structuring small units within Chronicles. These studies complement the thesis of this study in two ways. First, they highlight further the Chronicler's rhetorical skill. Secondly, several of these studies show that the devices support the themes which have been recognized in our statement of the Chronicler's purpose. Where particularly relevant, these studies will be referred to. However, the focus of the following examination will be on the overall structure of the historical narrative rather than on the structure of the many subunits.

2. Examination of the Structure

a. Thesis: David and Solomon as the Paradigm for Seeking Yahweh

On the surface structure of the narrative, the Chronicler has selected and structured his account of Judah's history in order to present a certain story-line or emplotment. In this story, the reigns of David and Solomon serve as an ideal type. This ideal type then functions as a paradigm to which the successive reigns of the Davidic kings were compared, and by which they were evaluated. The narrative emplotment also carries with it an argument about the course of history and the nature of reality. As a result, the audience is implicitly called on to accept an ideology about how to live in this reality. Inherent to the narrative is an attempt to persuade the audience to evaluate their present situation in light of this paradigm and to take appropriate action. The possibility of following the ideal model offers the audience the hope of blessing.

b. 1 Chronicles 1–9: The Introduction

Chronicles opens in chs. 1–9 with 'chronicle' material, that is, open-ended data without the inaugural, transitional and closing elements of a story. This material consists of various types of genealogies and lists, interspersed with some brief

---

[1] *Ibid.*, p. 16.

historical anecdotes and narrative comments. These chapters serve as the introduction to the total story of the Chronicler. They establish the principal subjects of the narrative, the theological concerns of the narrator, the general time parameters and the laws of reality at work within the story's world-view.[1]

Starting with creation and Adam, the Chronicler quickly funnels down his range of view temporally, geographically and nationally to a focus on the twelve sons of Israel (1 Chron. 2.1-2). Chapters 2–8 are devoted to the descendants of these sons and the land they possessed. However, great detail is given in these lists to two tribes: the sons of Judah (2.3–4.23), with particular interest devoted to the lineage of David (2.3-17) and the Davidic dynasty (3.1-24); and to the sons of Levi (6.1-80), with attention given to the Aaronic priesthood (6.1-15, 50-53) and the temple musicians (6.31-47). Thus the subjects of Judah, the Davidic monarchy, and the Jerusalem temple cultus have been introduced to the audience before the narrative proper begins. Also the genealogy of Benjamin, begun in 7.6-12, is repeated in a variant form in 8.29-40. Two results are achieved by this repetition: attention is directed to a tribe which became closely associated with Judah, and movement is made toward the opening of the narrative. From this tribe came the first Israelite king, Saul, with whom the narrative proper begins in ch. 10.[2] In 9.2-21 the genealogies record the first returning exiles to resettle the land after the Babylo-

---

1 The genealogies and lists of 1 Chronicles 1–9, in whole or part, have frequently been considered to be late insertions not originally belonging to the following narrative (see Welch, p. 1; Rudolph, *Chronikbücher*, pp. 1-2; Noth, *Studien*, pp. 112-22; Myers, *I Chronicles*, p. xli; and Cross, pp. 11-14). Even if this were the case, our thesis is not altered, for our interest is not in the history of the parts but in a synchronic reading of the whole; and, we have defined the 'Chronicler' as the major editor/composer of the final form. However, there is evidence that 1 Chron. 1–9 was deliberately composed as a part of the total work. William Osborne ('The Genealogies of 1 Chronicles 1–9' [Ph.D. dissertation; The Dropsie University, 1979]) has demonstrated a unity of subject matter, key words, motifs, and theology between these chapters and the narrative proper. So, too, Williamson (*Israel*, pp. 71-82) and Im (pp. 14-16) see chs. 1–9 as an integral part of the whole work.

2 Williamson (*1 and 2 Chronicles*, p. 46) notes that the most important post-exilic tribes (Judah, Levi and Benjamin) are placed at the beginning, middle and end respectively.

nian Captivity. The final temporal limit is thus hinted at as the return from exile, an event alluded to at the close of Chronicles (2 Chron. 36.20-23).

Interspersed among these lists lie brief narrative statements which signal to the audience the laws operating within the world of the narrative.[1] For example, those who are wicked in Yahweh's sight or who are unfaithful to him and worship other gods receive the curse of death or exile (2.3; 5.25-26; 9.1), but those who cry out to Yahweh and trust him are heard and receive Yahweh's helpful intervention (4.10; 5.20-22). These narrative statements reveal a world-view in which Yahweh is active in history. They reveal divine, causal laws operating in the world of the narrative, according to which blessing or punishment is meted out in response to certain types of human behavior.[2] Exposure to these laws or principles prepares the audience for a fuller presentation of the concept of seeking Yahweh which is developed and illustrated in the main narrative.

c. 1 Chronicles 10–2 Chronicles 9: Davidic and Solomonic Paradigm

In the narrative which follows the lists, the Chronicler painted a picture in which he portrayed David and Solomon as ones who properly sought Yahweh by instituting and upholding the official temple cultus.[3] First, though, a brief account of Saul is

---

[1] It is not the concern here to answer whether these narrative statements were created by the Chronicler or simply included as found. Actually, it is not uncommon for genealogies to contain such brief narration, and, it is possible that the material in these historical anecdotes came from ancient sources (R.W. Klein, pp. 1, 6, 10). Original, created or reshaped, the lists and genealogies suit the Chronicler's purposes.

[2] The principle of retribution has received recognition not only as a dominant motif, but also as a basis for structuring the narrative, particularly of the account of the Davidic kings. See: Osborne, pp. 38-51; Braun, 'Significance', p. 204; Dillard, 'Reward and Punishment', pp. 167-70; De Vries, chapter 4; and the following Section d, '2 Chronicles 10–36: The Davidic Kings'.

[3] The unity of the period of David and Solomon has also been observed and supported by R. Braun ('Solomonic Apologetic in Chronicles', *JBL* 92 [1973], pp. 503-16); Osborne (pp. 10-11); H.G.M. Williamson ('The Accession of Solomon in the Books of Chronicles', *VT* 26 [1976], pp. 356-

given in ch. 10. This portrayal of Saul sets him up as a foil for
David so that contrasts between the two may be drawn.[1] Saul
inquired (שאל) of a medium (10.13); David inquired (שאל) of
God (14.10, 11). Saul was defeated by the Philistines and his
head was placed in the temple of Dagon (10.1, 9-10). On the
other hand, Yahweh gave David victory over the Philistines
and their gods (ch. 14). All of Saul's house perished (10.6; note
that Mephibosheth is never mentioned in the narrative); but
David's lineage and claim to the kingdom were secured by
Yahweh (ch. 17). The ark was not sought in the days of Saul
(13.3), but David's first official act was to try to bring up the
ark to Jerusalem (ch. 13). Saul was put to death because he did
not keep the word of Yahweh and seek him (10.13-14),
whereas David's rule was secured because his actions exemplified the proper behavior. Again, the divine, causal laws of
the Chronicler's world-view are drawn on to explain Saul's
death and David's rise to kingship:

> Saul died because of his transgression which he transgressed
> against Yahweh, in that he did not keep the word of Yahweh,
> but even sought to inquire of a medium. Now he did not seek to
> inquire of Yahweh, so he put him to death, and he turned over
> the kingdom to David, the son of Jesse (1 Chron. 10.13-14).

With ch. 11, the attention turns to David. The account of David
is not in strict chronological order. It is structured to have a
rhetorical impact. Emphasized by means of an *inclusio* at

---

57); and Throntveit (pp. 114-15). Mosis, on the contrary, finds three
separate epochs which function paradigmatically: the account of Saul,
who serves as an example of one who did not do right; the period of
David, who began to do right and turn things around; and the account
of Solomon, who is the ideal king who established the ark in the
temple, but to whom none compared (pp. 164-204). Im (pp. 104-12), also
to the contrary, supports David alone as the model for the succeeding
kings.
[1] This feature has been noted by others including von Rad
(*Geschichtsbild*, p. 79), and Osborne (pp. 52-54). Seeing Saul as more
than just a foil for David, Ackroyd ('Exegete', pp. 3-9) and Mosis
(pp. 17-43) stress that the shift from Saul to David introduces a structural pattern for the Chronicler's history, a movement between exile
and restoration. Indeed, this pattern, which actually began in the
genealogies (noted also by Osborne, pp. 51-52), is part of the Chronicler's message about the results of seeking or not seeking Yahweh.

11.1-3 and 12.38-40, the narrator establishes in chs. 11–12 that 'all Israel' with one accord supported David's kingship, although he recognizes inside the bracketed material that military support actually came to David in stages (12.1, 16, 19, 23).[1] That David grew in grandeur because Yahweh was with him (11.9) is demonstrated by the excellence of the mighty men who gave their allegiance to him in this section. Secondly, in ch. 13, as his first official act, David brought up the ark of Yahweh. By such structuring of his account, the Chronicler conveys that the king chosen by Yahweh and endorsed by all the people was concerned first of all with establishing the proper worship of Yahweh—despite the fact that David's first attempt to bring up the ark actually met with failure.[2]

With the statement in 14.2, 'And David realized that Yahweh had *established* (כן) him as king over Israel and that his kingdom was exalted, for the sake of his people Israel', the Chronicler introduces to his audience a key term which clarifies a concept already manifest in his structure. This concept, which he will further demonstrate, is that there is a reciprocal bond between David's actions in 'establishing' the official cultic forms for worshipping Yahweh (1 Chron. 15.1, 3, 12; 22.3, 5, 14; 28.2; 29.2, 3, 19; 2 Chron. 1.4; 2.6) and Yahweh's promises and actions in regard to 'establishing' the Davidic kingdom (1

---

[1] Hugh Williamson ('Setting and Purpose', pp. 168-70) has further observed that this *inclusio* actually forms the outer frame of a chiastic structure which emphasizes David's coronation at its extremities and the support which came to him at his stronghold at its center.

[2] This change in chronological order has been widely observed (e.g. Osborne, p. 53). The rhetorical device of restructuring the order of events in order to emphasize the positive actions and character of a king is not unique to the Chronicler. Mordechai Cogan has identified in Assyrian records the practice of adjusting the chronology to date positive events early in a ruler's reign. He has noted that the Chronicler employed this structuring procedure in the reigns of Hezekiah and Josiah as well (M. Cogan, 'The Chronicler's Use of Chronology as Illuminated by Neo-Assyrian Royal Inscriptions', *Empirical Models for Biblical Criticism* [ed. J.H. Tigay; Philadelphia: University of Pennsylvania, 1985], pp. 197-209). John Van Seters (*In Search of History* [New Haven: Yale University Press, 1983], p. 36) has pointed out that in Herodotus an event may be reported out of chronological sequence in order that that event might serve as a model; the principle of analogy was more important than the principle of chronology.

Chron. 14.2; 17.11, 12, 14, 24; 22.10; 28.7). For example, the above declaration (14.2) accompanied by illustrations of David's successful rule in the rest of the chapter came after his attempt to bring the ark to Jerusalem (ch. 13). The scene found in the following chapters (15–16) again portrays David establishing the cult of Yahweh. The ark was successfully transported. David appointed Levitical singers and ministers. He led the people in worship. He set up everything 'according to all that is written in the law of Yahweh' (16.40b). This portrayal is followed by a scene in which David, desiring to build a house for Yahweh, receives the promise from Yahweh to 'establish' (כון) the Davidic dynasty (ch. 17). Chapters 18–20 then give illustrations of David's military success orchestrated by Yahweh in the establishment of David's kingdom, and resulting in the acquisition of wealth for the building of the temple (1 Chron. 18.11; 22.14; 29.3-5). The juxtaposition of these scenes is not accidental. They demonstrate the reciprocal link between David establishing Yahweh's cult and of Yahweh establishing David's kingdom. Tae-Soo Im has further observed that the connection between 'kingdom' and 'cult' was introduced with the account of Saul, who lost his kingdom because of his irreverent actions (ch. 10), and that the whole story of David was built upon this alternating pattern:[1]

1 Chronicles 11–12	Kingdom:	support of all Israel, Jerusalem established as the capital
1 Chronicles 13	Cult:	attempt to transport ark
1 Chronicles 14	Kingdom:	Yahweh gives military success
1 Chronicles 15–16	Cult:	David transports ark, appoints cultic officials
1 Chronicles 17–20	Kingdom:	military victories
1 Chronicles 21–29	Cult:	preparations for the temple

The Chronicler's only negative portrayal of David, and the only break in the paradigm, occurs in ch. 21. Here David committed the sinful act of numbering the people.[2] The

---

[1] Im, pp. 180-81.

[2] At least two significant differences are found between this version and the one in 2 Samuel 24. First, in Chronicles Satan ('the adversary') and not Yahweh incited David to this action. Second, Joab plays a more positive role in resisting David's desire for the census in

Chronicler lacks other traditions known from Samuel–Kings
which cast David in a negative light. Why, then, include this
account which threatens to weaken the paradigm? As has
been generally recognized, in this case the importance of one
theme outweighed the risk of weakening another. It was necessary to include this transgression of David in order not to
omit an event which was crucial in the founding of the
Jerusalem cult, for through this event the location for the altar
and temple was obtained.

With ch. 22 begins the account of David's preparations for
the temple (22.1-5, 14-16), preparations which continue
through ch. 29. Two sets of similar speeches by David in ch. 22
(vv. 6-16, 17-19) and ch. 28 (vv. 1-8, 9-10), form an *inclusio*
bracketing various temple concerns. Within these speech
forms,[1] the address calls for a response from the hearers sig-
nalled by the use of 'now' (עתה) or 'and now' (ועתה). The first
speech, addressed to Solomon, bases the succession of Solomon
to the throne on the word of Yahweh (v. 9) and requires the
response that Solomon build the temple and act in accord with
the laws of Yahweh in order to prosper (vv. 11-13). Although
the specific terms for 'establish' are not used, the principle of
the reciprocal relationship of 'establishing' is in force here. The
second speech, addressed to the leaders of Israel, requires that
they set their hearts to seek (דרש) Yahweh and build the temple (v. 19). The counterpart speeches in ch. 28 reveal an
inversion in the sequence of addressees and charges. This time
the divine confirmation of Solomon's succession is made to the

Chronicles. Again, it cannot be proven whether or not these differences came from the Chronicler's source or from his own hand. However, the first instance reflects a different theological perspective,
which perhaps developed under influences of the Persian period. The
second brings to light not a pro-Joab bias in Chronicles, but an anti-
Joab bias in 2 Samuel that perhaps was not present in the Chronicler's
source. Note that incidental details regarding Joab are present in the
Chronicler's account of the capture of Jebus (1 Chron. 11.4-9), which
are not mentioned in the account in 2 Samuel 5. These details in
Chronicles, which are favorable to Joab, do not appear to come from
any plan to elevate Joab. His role in Chronicles is minimal. In fact, if
anything, these details only detract from a more positive presentation
of David.
[1] See Newsome, pp. 210-13.

assembly of the leaders (vv. 1-7). David charges them to observe and seek (דרש) the commands of Yahweh (v. 8). In the address to Solomon, the principle of seeking is fully spelled out, 'if you seek him [Yahweh], he will let you find him; but if you forsake him, he will reject you forever' (v. 9), and Solomon is charged to take courage and build the temple (v. 10). The repetition of themes and addressees, along with the inversions, emphasize not just the Solomonic succession, but, more importantly, the relationship between seeking and blessing and the identification of seeking Yahweh with acts of establishing the cult.[1]

The bracketing effect of the speeches around chs. 23–27 also gives an added significance to the material in these chapters and further emphasis to the meaning of seeking Yahweh and his commandments. These chapters are often considered a late addition.[2] Whatever their literary history is, they have been integrated into the narrative by the bracketing effect of the speeches. They also serve an important role in the Chronicler's argument, since they are 'objective' lists testifying to David's acts of establishing the cultic institution. In these chapters are spelled out the various divisions and functions of the cultic personnel (chs. 23–26) and of the royal personnel (ch. 27), as they were appointed by David and the leaders (23.6; 24.3; 25.1). The appointments in these chapters, actually attributed to the final actions of David after Solomon was recognized as a king (cf. 23.1, 27), are out of chronological sequence with ch. 29 in which David turns the throne over to Solomon. As a result, the speeches about seeking and obeying Yahweh enclose material primarily of cultic concern. This structure also allows the account of David's life to close with speeches

---

[1] Braun ('Significance', pp. 205-207) has argued that chs. 22, 28, 29 form a transition from Davidic history to the history of Solomon. Hugh Williamson ('Accession', pp. 351-56) has further noted that this transition is modeled after the transition from Moses to Joshua found in Numbers and Deuteronomy.

[2] Welch, p. 81; Noth, *Studien*, pp. 112-13; Rudolph, *Chronikbücher*, pp. 3, 152.

which show his cultic concern and which stress the Chronicler's message.[1]

The first speech in ch. 28, already mentioned, serves another rhetorical function. It draws together past themes: David sought early in his reign to establish the cult by bringing up the ark (v. 2); he was a man of war (v. 3), a victorious one; the tribe of Judah was chosen to be a leader (v. 4); out of this tribe David was chosen to be king over all Israel (v. 4); Solomon was chosen to be the successor (vv. 5-6), establishing a principle of dynastic succession; and the people, too, were to seek Yahweh obediently (v. 8). By this means the narrator has both looked back and encapsulated the main themes of his story for his audience and has pointed forward to the role of Solomon. Chapters 28–29, which close with Solomon's popularly and divinely supported ascension to the throne (29.22b-25) and with David's death (29.26-30), also highlight cultic concerns: David gave to Solomon detailed plans for the temple (28.11-19); he commissioned Solomon and the people to the task of building the temple (28.20-21; 29.1-5); David gave of his wealth for the temple (29.2-5); the people responded wholeheartedly in their giving for the temple (29.6-9); David offered a prayer thanking Yahweh and requesting that Solomon and the people be given hearts directed toward God in obedience (29.10-19); and, the people responded by blessing Yahweh and rejoicing (29.20-22a).

The Chronicler's portrayal of David comprises about 28% of his total story about the history of Judah. At first glance one might suppose that the character of David was of particular importance to the Chronicler. Yet, in this material there is very little interest in the personality of David the man. In contrast to the account in Samuel–Kings, little is learned

---

[1] Because this deliberate structuring was not recognized, a later gloss was added in 29.22 in which Solomon is made king a second time (שׁנית). Leslie C. Allen (*The Greek Chronicles* [2 vols.; VTSup, 25, 27; Leiden: E.J. Brill, 1974]; vol. 2: *Textual Criticism*, p. 145) has noted that שׁנית was apparently not in the *Vorlage* belonging to the earliest Greek translations.

about David's thoughts and feelings.[1] In Chronicles he is David, the one who established the cultic forms of Yahweh worship and whose kingdom Yahweh established. Through his story of David, the Chronicler has set forth David as a model.[2] David is the ideal king who exemplified correct behavior before Yahweh. An important rhetorical impact in this typological presentation is not to be overlooked. David is not just a model to which the succeeding Davidic kings were to be compared. Implicitly, he also serves as a model for the Chronicler's audience of one who sought Yahweh.

Solomon followed in David's ways, carried out the construction of the temple, and completed the Chronicler's paradigm. Solomon's first official action was to worship Yahweh at the altar at Gibeon (2 Chron. 1.1-7). In return, Yahweh appeared there to Solomon and promised him wisdom, riches and honor (1.7-13)—the first of which is summarily illustrated in vv. 14-17. Solomon then completed David's plans for the temple and the cultus in 2 Chronicles 2–8: Solomon made preparations for building the temple with Hiram (ch. 2); the temple was built at the place which David had prepared (3.1–5.1); Solomon assembled all Israel for the transportation of the ark into the holy of holies amidst singing and celebration (5.2-14); he led the people in praise and in a dedicatory prayer (ch. 6); he and the people celebrated the dedication with sacrifices and feasting (7.1-10); and, in 8.12-15 Solomon put into motion the daily sacrifices and calendrical feasts and appointed the priestly and Levitical divisions according to David's ordinance. With a listing of Solomon's building projects (8.1-11) and an illustration of his wealth and wisdom (ch. 9), the account of Solomon comes to a close. So, too, does the narrator's paradigm. Solomon, who further established the cult of Yahweh ('Thus all of the work of Solomon was carried out from the day of the foundation of the house of Yahweh and until it was finished' [8.16]), was himself established by Yahweh.

---

[1] So, too, observed W. Johnstone, 'Guilt and Atonement: The Theme of 1 and 2 Chronicles', *A Word in Season* (ed. J.D. Martin and P.R. Davies; JSOTSup, 42; Sheffield: JSOT, 1986), p. 113.
[2] See below Section d, '2 Chronicles 10–36: The Davidic Kings'.

The structure of this account of Solomon further highlights the message of the Chronicler. In this section Raymond Dillard has uncovered a chiastic structure:[1]

A. Solomon's wealth and wisdom (1.1-17)
    (Trade in horses, 1.14-17)

  B. Recognition by gentiles/dealings with Hiram (2.1-16)
      (Yahweh's love for Israel, 2.11)

    C. Temple construction/gentile labor (2.17-5.1)
        (Gentile labor, 2.17-18)
        (Completion of temple, 5.1)

      D. Dedication of temple (5.2–7.10)

          1. a. Summons ⎫
             b. Sacrifice ⎬ 5.2-14
             c. Music ⎪
             d. Glory cloud ⎭

           2. Solomon speaks to the people (6.1-11)
              a. Exodus (6.5)
              b. Choice of Jerusalem (6.6-11)

           2′. Solomon speaks to God (6.12-42)
              a. Promises to David (6.16-17)
              b. Eyes open; hear and forgive (6.18-42)

         1′. d. Glory cloud ⎫
             c. Music ⎬ 7.1-10
             b. Sacrifice ⎪
             a. Dismissal ⎭

      D′. Divine response (7.11-22)

        [1. not present]

          2. God speaks to Solomon (7.12-18)
              b. Eyes open; hear and forgive (7.13-16)
              a. Promises to David (7.19-21)

          2′. God speaks to the people (7.19-22)
              b. Choice of Jerusalem (7.19-21)
              a. Exodus (7.22)

        [1′. not present]

    C′. Other construction/gentile labor (8.1-16)
        (Gentile labor, 8.7-10)
        (Completion of temple, 8.16)

  B′. Recognition by gentiles/dealings with Hiram (8.17–9.12)
      (Yahweh's love for Israel, 9.8)

A′. Solomon's wealth and wisdom (9.13-28)
    (Trade in horses, 9.25-28)

---

1 Dillard, 'Literary Structure', pp. 87-88.

One might modify Dillard's outline slightly. Since patterns of alternation (1 2 1 2) can also take place within elements of a generally chiastic pattern, there is no need to seek a 'perfect' chiasm as Dillard does. For myself, I see only one 'D' section structured as follows.

    D. Dedication of temple and divine response (5.2–7.22)

        1. Physical acts of dedication (5.2-14)
            a. Summons
            b. Sacrifice
            c. Music
            d. Glory cloud

        2. Addresses by Solomon (6.1-42)
            a. To the people
            b. To God

        1'. Physical acts of dedication (7.1-10)
            d. Glory cloud
            c. Music
            b. Sacrifice
            a. Dismissal

        2'. Addresses by God (7.11-22)
            b. To Solomon
            a. To the people

What is significant with either of the above outlines is that the focal point, the center element/s (D above, or D and D' in Dillard's) is the dedication of the temple of Yahweh. This is the Chronicler's main point of emphasis when telling the story of Solomon. Also to be noticed is the fact that the outer elements of the structure (A and B) illustrate the establishment of Solomon's kingdom, while the inner element (D) portrays Solomon's establishment of cult of Yahweh, the two main structuring elements of the history of David.[1]

Two other themes found earlier in the account of David receive further emphasis and expansion in the section on the dedication of the temple. First, the conditional nature of the agreement with David, which was only briefly stated before

[1] It is interesting to note that although there is a contrast between the 'C' elements (the first 'C' records sacred building and 'C'' records secular building), 'C'' closes with a reference to the temple building (8.16) that parallels the closing of 'C' (5.1).

(1 Chron. 22.13; 28.7), is repeated and expanded in 2 Chron. 6.16 and 7.17-22. Secondly, in Solomon's prayer of dedication, the Chronicler's principle of seeking/forsaking Yahweh is repeated and expanded. This principle now includes a related concept: if one comes under Yahweh's wrath and then humbles oneself and again turns to Yahweh, that person will be restored (2 Chron. 7.18-39). Both of these themes reveal that the principle of retribution is not fatalistic; rather, they stress the element of human responsibility. Blessing is not permanent; it is dependent on responsible behavior toward Yahweh. Neither is cursing permanent; it can be reversed by Yahweh who restores the humble. Through these themes the narrator has further foreshadowed things to come and prepared the audience for the pattern of reversals in judgment and blessing that occur among the Davidic kings.

As with the portrayal of David, that of Solomon is positive and idealistic. Together with the inaugural material (1 Chron. 1–9), the narrative concerning David and Solomon makes up 49% of the total work. Once again there is little to be learned about Solomon the man. Rather, Solomon is the one who fulfilled the plans for the temple and the cultic practices and whom Yahweh blessed with wealth, wisdom and peace.

d. 2 Chronicles 10–36: The Davidic Kings

Having established his paradigm, the Chronicler next presented the accounts of the kings of Judah in quick succession. He both illustrated his model further through his account of their lives, and evaluated them in terms of this model. Jehoshaphat, Ahaz, Hezekiah and Josiah are explicitly compared to David and/or Solomon (17.3; 28.1; 29.2; 34.2, 3). Other comparisons are implicit. If a king 'does right in the sight of Yahweh', 'walks in the ways' of a righteous predecessor, humbles himself, preserves the Jerusalem cult (i.e. engages in some form of seeking Yahweh), then the king is blessed with deliverance from defeat, with military success, wealth, building projects and so forth. If the king 'walks in the ways' of an unrighteous predecessor, is proud, relies on an idolatrous king or nation, ignores cultic concerns (i.e. some expression of forsaking Yahweh), then he and the people meet with a reversal of fate.[1] Again this observation is not new. Osborne, in his dissertation, found this section highly structured:

> The second half of the Chronicler's composition is constructed of a series of narratives that have several key motifs, the number of which may vary in any given narrative, although the arrangement has a distinct pattern and order of appearance. When counted, there are seven characteristic motifs.[2]

The seven motifs he identified are: (1) the seeking motif, which is sometimes stated in the evaluation of a monarch, sometimes woven into the narrative, and sometimes implicit; (2) religious acts (cultic or legal) of a monarch, which are usually found at the beginning of an account; (3) military mobilization, that is, the ability of a king to build fortifications and muster troops if he has sought Yahweh; (4) military engagement, which results in victory when the king is obedient, and in defeat when disobedient; (5) prophetic speech, which sets the stage for the next element in the Chronicler's illustration of his salvation theology; (6) the response of king or people to prophetic speech (obedience, repentance, disbelief, disobedience); and (7) God's judgment on the basis of the response.[3] It should be noted that all of Osborne's elements belong to what Schaefer and this writer have referred to as the principle or paradigm of 'seeking Yahweh', the primary argument of which the Chronicler strove to persuade his audience. The examples of the three kings immediately following Solomon illustrate the structuring which occurs around this principle.

Rehoboam began his reign well. He obeyed Yahweh and, therefore, was able to establish a strong kingdom (11.1, 5-12, 18-23). Later, he and all Israel forsook Yahweh. As a consequence, they suffered under the forces of Shishak of Egypt. When they humbled themselves, the situation was reversed and they were restored (12.1-12). On the whole, the Chroni-

---

[1] See the chart of the signs of blessing and punishment at the end of this chapter.

[2] Osborne, p. 39.

[3] *Ibid.*, pp. 39-46. The Chronicler, according to Osborne, may omit an element or change the order of these elements (p. 46).

cler evaluated Rehoboam as one who did not set his heart to seek Yahweh (12.13).

Abijah maintained the Jerusalem cult (13.10-11). Therefore, he was successful in battle when he and the people cried to Yahweh and trusted in him (13.13-20).

Asa removed foreign cult places and, along with the people of Judah, sought Yahweh. His reign was first marked by building projects, military success and eventually by rest from his enemies (chs. 14–15). Later he failed to rely on Yahweh and to seek him (ch. 16). His military success was then hindered (16.7), and he became diseased (16.12, 13). In this account, the principle of seeking Yahweh is directly announced to Asa by the prophet Azariah, in 15.2. By this means, the audience also is again reminded of the operative principle in the Chronicler's narrative world.

This format continues down to the reign of Zedekiah. Not only did this king harden his heart against Yahweh, but even the officials of the priests and the people committed abominations. They defiled the house of Yahweh and they rejected the messages of the prophets, until there was no remedy. The temple was destroyed and the people were carried off into captivity (36.11-21).

It should be noted that there are cases in which the Chronicler had difficulty reconciling his model of history to the traditions with which he apparently assumed his audience was familiar. For example, the Chronicler could not blame the division of the kingdom under Rehoboam on the transgressions of Solomon, as the tradition in 1 Kings 11 does. This would call his paradigm of a faithful Solomon into question. Instead, he directed attention to the harshness of Rehoboam's behavior as if it were the cause for the division. Although alluding to the prophecies which were in response to Solomon's transgressions (10.15; 11.4), the Chronicler simply stated that God caused his word to be established through Rehoboam's behavior. Another example is found in the account of Rehoboam. Even though he humbled himself when oppressed by Shishak, his deliverance was not complete (12.6-12). Why was he not completely delivered and granted victory over the Egyptians? The Chronicler explains that Yahweh chose this way of *partial* deliverance so that he and the people might learn a lesson about serving Yahweh (12.6-7). Despite these occasional difficulties, the Chronicler continued to employ his paradigm very consistently throughout his history of Judah.

3. *Analysis of the Structure*
To the purists, the following analysis might step beyond the usual bounds of a rhetorical analysis and move into the area of 'poetics'. Aristotle analyzed the art of poetics as a distinct subject in its own right.[1] However, this writer believes that this step does not take one far from the realm of Aristotle's approach to rhetoric. He recognized that narration in a speech should make use of the modes of persuasion to move the audience.[2] And, although in this first analysis reference will not be made to the three modes of persuasion, our concern is still to observe how the structure of the Chronicler's story would have contributed to communicating his purpose persuasively.

All narratives are emplotted in some way. They relate a story-line and present to the audience a kind of story. What impact does structuring the story of Judah around the Chronicler's paradigm have on the overall story-line or emplotment in Chronicles? What kind of story has been told?

When the story in Chronicles is viewed as a whole, one notices very little development of a main plot through such devices as tension and resolution. One might say that there is some movement in the overall story from the establishment of the official cultus and Davidic dynasty to their virtual demise at the end of the story. Still, there is very little development of an an overall story-line. Rather there exist a long story about the founding of the cult under David and Solomon and shorter stories about individual kings. To borrow an analogy from the realm of photography, one might say that each story about a Davidic monarch functions as a still photograph, a separate 'frame' of history which is juxtaposed to the next 'frame'. Developments of tensions and resolutions occur within each frame, but they do not move a greater story along. Other than the temporal, linear succession of rulers, each frame has

---

[1] See Aristotle, *Poetics*.
[2] Aristotle, *Rhetoric*, III. 16.

almost no impact on what precedes and follows it. Each king receives recompense for his own actions. What dominates is the repetition of the paradigmatic principle in scene after scene. Such structuring conveys an evaluation and explanation not just of the course of Judean history, but also of the present reality that the Chronicler shared with his audience. What impact, then, does such as story have on an audience? What does it convey about the ideology and world-view within the narrative world?

a. *Structure and the Laws of Reality*
Within the Chronicler's world-view certain divinely ordained causal laws of reality are in effect. The Chronicler's narrative structure reveals something about how these laws operate. The operation of these laws is basically contained within the parameters of each 'frame'. Von Rad made a similar observation when he stated:

> [I]n proportion as the Chronicler strove to assign to each generation complete immediacy to Jahweh, he lost sight of the understanding of the history of Israel as a unity... His picture threatens to disintegrate into a large number of single actions of Jahweh.[1]

I would suggest that the Chronicler did not lose sight of 'the history of Israel as a unity', but saw the history of Israel as exhibiting a certain understanding about reality which he sought to convey in his narrative reconstruction.

By arrangement of the elements in his story into disconnected pictures, he represents a world-view in which the laws of reality hold true within relatively short temporal and subject parameters. They are not laws which govern the course of the world as if it were a single entity; rather, they govern the smaller units of the course of each generation. The significance of this structuring can be seen more clearly when one contrasts the Chronicler's story-line to that found in Samuel–Kings. In that tradition there is a continuous story-line which runs on an ever downward course. The causal laws at work within Samuel–Kings are similar to those in Chronicles but

[1] Von Rad, *Old Testament Theology* (2 vols.; trans. D.M.G. Stalker; New York; Harper & Row, 1962, 1965), 1.350.

operate in a more linear and mechanistic manner. As a result, Samuel–Kings presents a fairly fatalistic world-view. Particularly from the reign of Manasseh onwards, the fate of Judah was sealed (2 Kgs 21.10-15). The course of the nation was a tragic one, ending with the curse of Yahweh being carried out.

The Chronicler, however, tells a different story. The course of history is not so predetermined. Within his representation of reality, reversal of negative or positive situations could take place within a given reign or from one reign to the next.[1] The potential for change always existed. Further, the principles at work in the world are usually put into motion by the human element, the Davidic king and the people of Judah as a whole. As a result, it is the human element that is portrayed as responsible for its own consequences, not some capricious god.[2] A speech on the lips of Hezekiah provides a good illustration of these points:

> Listen to me, O Levites. Consecrate yourselves now... and carry the uncleanness out from the holy place. For our fathers have been unfaithful and have done evil in the sight of Yahweh our God... Therefore the wrath of Yahweh was against Judah and Jerusalem... Now it is in my heart to make a covenant with Yahweh God of Israel, that his burning anger may turn away from us. My sons, do not be negligent now... (2 Chron. 29.5-11).

The 'fathers' came under the wrath of Yahweh for their unfaithfulness, but this did not mean that Hezekiah's generation, too, was condemned to suffer. Rather, he was able to offer hope to his generation. If they would seek Yahweh by restoring the cultic institutions, wrath would be turned away from them. (Only at the end of Chronicles does one find a cumula-

---

[1] Osborne (pp. 51-57) identified two patterns in which contrasts between reward and punishment are illustrated, either by contrasting the stories of two successive kings (Saul and David, Jehoram and Joash, Ahaz and Hezekiah, Amon and Josiah) or by showing a reversal in the life of the same king (Rehoboam, Asa, Jehoshaphat, Joash, Amaziah, Uzziah and Manasseh).

[2] As remarked above, the Chronicler has some difficulty accounting for the division of the kingdom under Rehoboam. He focuses on the behavior not of Solomon, but of Rehoboam, yet notes that Rehoboam's actions fulfilled the prophetic word of Yahweh (2 Chronicles 10, particularly v. 15).

tive and irremediable effect of forsaking Yahweh [2 Chron. 36.15-17], and even this judgment was to last only seventy years until restoration took place for the next generation.) Therefore, the Chronicler's structure communicates that history is not locked into a fatalistic course. Hope for restored blessing in times of judgment is ever present.

b. *Character Portrayal and Classification*
By his choice and arrangement of material, the Chronicler has created stereotypical portrayals of the kings of Judah. He has not always ordered events chronologically, but in such a way as to convey his assessment of each king, an assessment he wished the audience to accept. Material in the lives of David and Solomon has been particularly chosen and arranged with care to present a certain image of these characters who sought Yahweh. For the Chronicler, David and Solomon became model characters who belonged to Israel's 'Golden Age'. They achieved wealth, fame, wisdom, military success and a dynastic kingdom. Under them all Israel prospered, because they sought Yahweh, depended upon him, and established the proper institutions for worshiping him. David and Solomon are 'heroes' who rose above the 'darker side of life' (as Saul did not) and obtained success/blessing. Of the succeeding kings, those that chose to follow the model of the founding heroes also received blessing; those who did not received retribution. The lives of these kings were treated individually as separate units, but not for the purpose of demonstrating their unique personalities and human characteristics. They are portrayed typologically. The accounts of their lives were reduced to details which relate to the principle of seeking. This reduction serves the purpose of classification. Each king can be classified as one who did or did not seek Yahweh. The simplicity and clarity of the portrayals are intended to move the audience to accept the Chronicler's judgment of each past king and his generation.

Does such an implicit invitation to evaluate and classify direct one's attention solely to the kings and to the past? How might such an invitation impact an audience in a post-exilic situation without a Davidic monarch? First, one should recognize that the kings were naturally the point of attention for the Chronicler. They sat on Yahweh's throne.[1] They represented the people in corporate petition before Yahweh.[2] The consequences of their behavior in regard to the worship of Yahweh impacted the well-being of the nation.[3] They exercised the power over the cult of Yahweh, to tear it down (e.g. Ahaz and Manasseh) or to re-establish it (e.g. Hezekiah and Josiah). And, their leadership did influence the responses of the people.[4] Secondly, however, one should note that the Chronicler made it clear that the principle of seeking Yahweh applied to 'all Israel' and not exclusively to the kings. The historical anecdotes in the genealogies, which first introduced the principle to the audience, applied it broadly. Moreover, in the accounts of the Davidic kings, the people, too, are credited with acting either responsibly or irresponsibly.[5] In fact, in a couple of instances, the people are culpable when the king is innocent.[6] Prophetic speeches also address the people, thus revealing their accountability.[7] Therefore, each generation, although tending to follow the lead of their rulers, shared in the responsibility for the state of their current circumstances.

It appears, then, that the impact of the Chronicler's reduction and structuring would be to induce the audience to take another step and to evaluate and classify the character and situation of their own generation. They should be moved to self-analysis. Even if they no longer have a Davidic king, they still have the cult of Yahweh. Are they the ones who have sought Yahweh and cared for the cultic institutions? What does their current situation reveal as the answer? Further, the audience, who presumably also want success, are implicitly called on by such 'negative–positive' depictions to emulate the

---

[1] 1 Chron. 17.14; 28.5; 29.23; 2 Chron. 9.8. For further observations regarding this point, see Im (pp. 164-67).

[2] 2 Chron. 6.18-42; 14.11; 20.5-12.

[3] 2 Chron. 12.5; 16.7-9; 32.24-25.

[4] 2 Chron. 14.4; 15.9-15; 19.4; 20.4; 20.20-21; 21.11; 28.19; 32.6-8; 33.9, 16; 34.33.

[5] 2 Chron. 11.3-4; 11.16-17; 13.14; 15.9-15; 20.18; 23.16; 24.17-21; 24.24; 28.6; 36.14-16.

[6] 2 Chron. 27.2; 34.24-28.

[7] 2 Chron. 11.3-4; 15.1-2; 20.14-15; 24.20; 36.23 (by Cyrus).

heroes of the story and to eschew the behavior of the villains.

c. *Summary*

The presentation of a master paradigm and a type of structuring which reduced each element in the historical field and compared it to the master paradigm for classification implicitly invites the audience to judge the past for themselves. They are also led to evaluate the present in terms of the past. Having made an evaluation, they are not left in despair of being locked into an unchangeable situation. There are causal laws operating within reality which can effect the reversal of one's own situation and which are put into effect by human agency. The course of action that operates within these laws and achieves success/blessing has also been communicated. They can model their actions after the archetypal figures of David and Solomon. Both by the narrative content and structure the audience is not only presented with an ideology of ethical/religious values, but also are moved, hopefully, to believe that it is profitable to act upon them. An attempt has been made to persuade the audience to take a proper course of action. The Chronicler offers to them the hope of blessing, if they too will conform to the paradigm. In this manner the Chronicler has striven to motivate his audience to trust in Yahweh and to establish and maintain the proper cultic worship in its day.

D. *Type of Rhetoric*

Chronicles, although not a speech, can be related to Aristotle's three types of rhetoric, which correspond to the purpose of a speech: (1) deliberative or political, (2) legal or forensic, and (3) epideictic or ceremonial.[1] Chronicles most closely functions as deliberative rhetoric, although it should not be overlooked that it employs elements found within all three divisions. In accord with the aim of epideictic speech, one finds that the Chronicler portrays the main characters of his story in such a way as to establish each character's honor or disrepute before the eyes of the audience. And, like legal speech, the actions of the characters and the events that take place are set before the audience

---

[1] See Chapter 1 D 4, 'Types of Rhetorical Speech'.

to be judged as right or wrong. Still, the overarching goal appears to be that of deliberative speech. The political orator addresses matters over which people deliberate, matters over which they have the ability to set into motion a course of action. Aristotle stated the general aim of political rhetoric thus:

> The political orator aims at establishing the expediency or the harmfulness of a proposed course of action; if he urges acceptance, he does so on the ground that it will do good; if he urges its rejection, he does so on the ground that it will do harm; and all other points, such as whether the proposal is just or unjust, honourable or dishonourable, he brings in as subsidiary and relative to this main consideration.[1]

In Aristotle's treatise one finds the following characteristics of deliberative or political speech:

1. There are five main concerns over which all people deliberate and on which political speakers make speeches: ways and means, war and peace, national defence, imports and exports, and legislation.[2] That is to say, on a broad level, it deals with those matters that determine the welfare of a nation.

2. Deliberative rhetoric uses 'narration' (*diēgēsis*), a survey of actions, for a particular purpose. In judicial speech one usually seeks to prove that past actions have taken place or that they were of a certain quality or extent. In ceremonial speech, 'narration' might be used to show that one's hero is brave or just. Deliberative speech, since it focuses on the future, usually will not depend on 'narration'. However, there are cases in which deliberative speech will use 'narration': 'If there is narration at all, it will be of past events, the recollection of which is to help the hearers to make better plans for the future'.[3]

---

[1] Aristotle, I. 3. 1358b.
[2] Aristotle, I. 4. 1359b.
[3] Aristotle, III. 16. 1417b13-14. However, Aristotle goes on to say, 'Or it [narration] may be employed to attack someone's character, or to eulogize him—only then you will not be doing what the political speaker, as such, has to do' (III. 16. 1417b15-17). As this last statement of Aris-

3. This type of rhetoric also tends to rely more on an inductive type of rational demonstration. '"Examples" are most suitable to deliberative speeches; for we judge of future events by divination from past events.'[1] 'Argument by "example" is highly suitable for political oratory, argument by "Enthymeme"[2] better suits forensic. Political oratory deals with future events, of which it can do no more than quote past events as examples.'[3]

4. Deliberative rhetoric has a specific premise and aim. The political rhetor argues from the premise that by adopting the recommended measures the end result will be greater good or 'happiness'.[4] 'Now the political or deliberative orator's aim is utility: deliberation seeks to determine not ends but the means to ends, i.e. what it is most useful to do.'[5]

One finds the above characteristics of deliberative speech in the books of Chronicles: the Chronicler was concerned about the national interests of Israel; he used 'narration' for the purpose of recollecting past events; these past events function as the examples of a inductive argument through which the Chronicler demonstrated what measures effected the national well-being; and, his argument spelled out the specific kind of action which would result in the good of the people. For the Chronicler, the nation's proper relationship to Yahweh was the factor which determined the status of matters of national interest. Seeking and obeying Yahweh brought about national well-being. The converse brought about disaster. In short, a deliberative rhetor seeks to inform the audience about those actions which will result in their greater good or happiness and to move them to take those actions. This is what it appears the Chronicler intended to do, so that, having learned

totle indicates, there can be some overlap in the methods and goals of the three types of oratory.

[1] Aristotle, I. 9. 1368a.

[2] The enthymeme and the example are described in Chapter 3.

[3] Aristotle, II. 17. 1418a1-2.

[4] Aristotle, I. 4-5. 1360b.

[5] Aristotle, I. 6. 1362a.

from the past, the people could pursue the correct course of behavior in their present circumstances.

IMPLICIT COMPARISONS
'SIGNS OF BLESSING AND CURSING'

Reigns	Military Success [1]	Building Projects	Large Army/ Fortifications	Popular Support [2]	Peace/ Rest	Prosperity/ Might [3]	Point of Reversal		Military Failure	Lost Support	Illness/ Death [4]
							Forsook	Humbled			
Genealogies I 1-9	5.20-22								5.25-26 9.1		II 3
Saul I 10									10.1-6		10.6, 13-14 I 21
David and Solomon I 11–II 9	14.8-16 18.1-20.8	I 14.1 I 15.1 II 2.1 II 8.1-6	I 11-12 I 18.6, 13 II 1.14	I 11-12 29.23-24	I 22.18 I 23.25	I 14.2 I 29.2-5, 23, 28, 30 II 1.1, 15 9.13, 14, 22	[I 21.1]	[I 21.16-17]			
Rehoboam II 10-12	[12.7-8]	11.5-12	11.1, 11-12	11.13-17		12.1, 13	12.1	12.6	12.2-4 (12.9)		
Abijah II 13	13.13-18			[13.10]		13.21					
Asa II 14-16	14.9-15 16.6	14.6-7 16.6	14.8	[14.4, 11] 15.9-15	14.4-7 15.15, 19	14.7	16.7		16.7-9	[16.10]	16.12
Jehoshaphat II 17-20	[18.31] 20.2-30	17.12	17.2, 12.19	17.5 [19.4] [20.3-4]	17.10 20.30	17.5, 12 18.1					
Jehoram II 21									[21.8-10] 21.16-17	21.19-20	21.12-15, 18-19
Ahaziah II 22.1-9											22.4, 7-9
(Athaliah) (II 22.9–23.21)										23.1-7	23.14-15
Joash II 24		24.13						24.18, 20, 24	24.23-24	24.25-26	24.25

Reigns	Military Success [1]	Building Projects	Large Army / Fortifications	Popular Support [2]	Peace / Rest	Prosperity / Might [3]	Point of Reversal Forsook	Humbled	Military Failure	Lost Support	Illness / Death [4]
Amaziah II 25	25.11-13		25.5-6				25.14-15		25.17-24	25.27-28	25.27
Uzziah II 26	26.6-8	26.2, 6 9-10	26.11-15	26.1		26.5, 8, 13, 15	26.16				26.16-23
Jotham II 27	27.5-7	27.3-4	27.4			27.6					
Ahaz II 28									28.5-8, 16-20		
Hezekiah II 29-32	32.20-22	32.5, 29-30	32.5	[29.36] [30.1-26]	32.22 [LXX]	31.21 32.23, 27-29	[32.25]	[32.26]			
Mannaseh II 33.1-20		33.14	33.14	[33.16]				33.12	33.10-11		
Amon II 33.21-25										33.24	
Josiah II 34-35				[34.29-33] 35.24-25			[35.20-22]		35.20-24		35.23-24
Jehoahaz/ Jehoiakim/ Jehoiachin/ Zedekiah II 36									36.3-4, 6-7, 10, 17-20		

[1] For the principle of military success/failure, see 1 Chron. 4.10; 2 Chron. 6.36; 13.12; 25.7-8.
[2] Popular support is generally indicated implicitly.
[3] For the principle of prosperity/might, see 1 Chron. 29.12; 2 Chron. 1.11-12
[4] God also prevents death (II 18.31) and heals illness (II 32.24).

Chapter 3

LOGOS: THE RATIONAL MODE OF PERSUASION

A. *Introduction to Aristotle's Concept*

According to Aristotle the rhetor has three means or modes of effecting persuasion internal to the communication itself: the first, typically designated 'ethos', is the appeal to the character of the speaker; the second, 'pathos', is the appeal to the emotions of the audience; and the third, usually called 'logos', is the rational appeal through the speech itself as it demonstrates the argument. The term 'logos', as a designation of the third mode, comes from Aristotle's initial description of these modes. There he stated that the third mode takes place *en autǭ tǭ logǭ to dia tou deiknynai ē phainesthai deiknynai*, that is, 'in/by the speech/word itself through proving or appearing to prove'.[1] While 'logos' in this phrase does not mean literally the 'rational' or the 'logical', but rather 'word/speech', the mode of persuasion it designates is one which takes place on the rational level. This is because the act of rhetorical 'proving' or 'demonstrating' (for which Aristotle uses *deiknynai* and *apodeiknynai*) is analogous to the logical argumentation of dialectic.[2]

---

[1] Aristotle, I. 2. 1356a3-4.
[2] This writer wishes to avoid giving the impression in the description of the modes of persuasion that reason (*logos*) is pitted against emotion (*pathos* and *ethos*). One should observe that Aristotle did not see a dichotomy between reason and emotion. Rather, where he sets forth his systematic treatment of the modes of persuasion, it is evident that they work together to achieve their effect. Vernon Robbins ('Rhetorical Arguments in Galatians 5–6' [paper presented at Emory University, October 1985]), in a succinct definition of the three modes, has captured the intricate relationship among them: '*Ethos* is the credibility of the speaker as manifested in the speech; *logos* is the speech which

In dialectic, according to Aristotle, there are two forms of demonstration or proof, one deductive, called the 'syllogism', and the other inductive, called simply, 'induction'. Correspondingly, in rhetoric there are two forms of demonstration, the enthymeme and the example. Aristotle stated:

> With regard to the persuasion achieved by proof or apparent proof: just as in dialectic there is induction on the one hand and syllogism or apparent syllogism on the other, so it is in rhetoric. The example is an induction, the Enthymeme is a syllogism. I call the Enthymeme a rhetorical syllogism, and the example a rhetorical induction. Every one who effects persuasion through proof does in fact use either Enthymemes or examples; there is no other way... When we base the proof of a proposition on a number of similar cases, this is induction in dialectic, example in rhetoric; when it is shown that, certain propositions being true, a further and quite distinct proposition must also be true in consequence, whether invariably or usually, this is called syllogism in dialectic, Enthymeme in rhetoric.[1]

In brief, the two forms of rhetorical demonstration may be defined as follows: The 'enthymeme' is an inferential argument which states some conviction regarding human affairs and a reason why this conviction should be accepted.[2] The reason supporting this enthymeme is generally based on probabilities or popular opinion. Enthymemes, in contrast to dialectical syllogisms, are evaluated in terms of being convincing or unconvincing; whereas dialectical syllogisms are evaluated in terms of being formally valid or invalid.[3] The 'example' is a form of argument where a parallel is drawn between things of the same class.[4]

To help clarify the distinction between examples and enthymemes in Chronicles, it should be noted that they occur in different kinds of narrative material. Examples occur in what might be called 'straight narrative', narrative material

functions credibly, and *pathos* is acceptance by the audience of the personal performance as credible'.

[1] Aristotle, I. 2. 1356a36-1356b17.
[2] For a fuller treatment, see E.E. Ryan, *Aristotle's Theory of Rhetorical Argumentation* (Montreal: Bellarmin, 1984), pp. 95-96.
[3] Ryan, p. 55.
[4] For a fuller description of the example, see Ryan (pp. 117-27).

which simply reports an event. Enthymemes occur in material in which an opinion or evaluation is stated either in speech
material by a character of the story or by the narrator in
'narrative comments'. In some cases the evaluative comments may be so woven into the telling of an event that it
becomes difficult to separate cleanly the two forms of argumentation.

B. *Application to Chronicles*

The following analysis of the 'rational' mode of persuasion in
Chronicles seeks to accomplish three objectives: (1) to demonstrate how the Chronicler's argument for seeking Yahweh is
presented in the forms of the enthymeme and the example; (2)
to identify the material and logical structures upon which the
rational argument is constructed; and (3) to show how the
enthymeme and example are developed and arranged in a
complementary manner in Chronicles in order to effect persuasion.

1. *Demonstration through the Enthymeme and the Example*
a. *The Argument*
How, then, are the enthymeme and the example employed in
the Chronicler's demonstration of his argument? For the purpose of this analysis of Chronicles, it has been supposed that
G.E. Schaefer in his dissertation, 'The Significance of Seeking
God in the Purpose of the Chronicler', has formulated well one
of the main purposes of the Chronicler's narrative, one that is
promoted on the level of narrative emplotment. Schaefer has
demonstrated that the Chronicler, using many means of conveying the message, wished to inculcate in his audience a
theology of 'seeking Yahweh'.[1] In general, to seek Yahweh
according to the Chronicler meant to worship Yahweh rather
than other gods, to turn to Yahweh in trust, and to obey him.
But, more particularly, properly seeking Yahweh included
establishing and maintaining the Yahwistic cultic system of
worship centered at the temple in Jerusalem. The message the
Chronicler conveyed on the level of emplotment was that

---

[1] See Chapter 2 B, 'A Purpose of the Chronicler'.

seeking Yahweh through the proper cultic means resulted in
blessing, while forsaking Yahweh or failing to seek him
resulted in being forsaken by Yahweh. This principle is
explicitly argued as operative in the lives of those the Chronicler described. And by implication, it is a vital message which
he desired his audience to accept and upon which he desired
them to act.

b. *Illustration of the Enthymeme*[1]

An illustration of the enthymematic form of the argument is
found in a narrative comment immediately following the
straight narration of Saul's death (1 Chron. 10.1-12):

> And Saul died for his sin which he sinned against Yahweh on
> account of the word of Yahweh which he did not keep, and even
> by asking the medium to seek. But he did not seek Yahweh, so
> he killed him and he turned over the kingdom to David the son of
> Jesse (vv. 13-14).

The enthymeme presented in this narrative evaluation,
expressed in its negative form, is: Saul died and lost his kingdom, because he did not seek Yahweh. Although the enthymeme is complete in this form, it can be restated as a dialectical syllogism:

> The one who does not seek Yahweh will be punished.
> Saul did not seek Yahweh.
> Therefore, Saul was punished (lost his kingdom and his life).

A statement does not have to include all of the elements of a
formal syllogism to be recognized as an enthymeme. Various
elements may be left implicit, when the rhetor believes these
elements to be understood by the audience. Either of the
premises in the above syllogism may omitted. In our text (1
Chron. 10.13-14), the first premise, a general principle of
divine retribution, is left unstated, but is assumed to be understood by the audience. Also, the term 'punished/punishment' is
not stated, for the Chronicler is implying that loss of one's
kingdom and/or life in military defeat is in this case a sign of

---

[1] See Lists 1 and 2 in the Appendix for a listing of the enthymemes
related to the principle of seeking Yahweh.

divine punishment.[1] Then, too, the specific application, the second premise, may be omitted and the general principle of the 'seeking' argument stated alone, in negative or positive form: 'If you seek him [Yahweh], he will let you find him; but if you forsake him, he will reject you forever' (1 Chron. 28.9-10). Again, this could be restated: A person is blessed (i.e. 'finds' Yahweh), because/if that person seeks Yahweh.

c. *Illustration of the Example*

An illustration of the same argument, but in the inductive form of an example, may be found in the narration of an event concerning Rehoboam in 2 Chron. 12.1-8:

> It took place when the kingdom of Rehoboam was established and strong that he and all Israel with him forsook the law of Yahweh. And it came about in King Rehoboam's fifth year, because they had been unfaithful to Yahweh, that Shishak king of Egypt came up against Jerusalem... And he captured the fortified cities of Judah and came as far as Jerusalem. Then Shemaiah the prophet came to Rehoboam and the leaders of Judah who had gathered at Jerusalem because of Shishak, and he said to them, 'Thus say Yahweh, "You have forsaken me, so I also have forsaken you to Shishak"'. So the leaders of Israel and the king humbled themselves and said, 'Yahweh is righteous'. And when Yahweh saw that they humbled themselves, the word of Yahweh came to Shemaiah, saying, 'They have humbled themselves so I will not destroy them, but I will grant them some deliverance, and my wrath shall not be poured out on Jerusalem by means of Shishak'.

One should note that not only are both the negative and positive expressions of the seeking principle present (punishment and blessing), but also in the middle of the narration, the argument is stated in enthymematic form in the exhortation of Shemaiah the prophet (vv. 5, 7).

Another example, without the presence of the interpretive enthymeme, is found in the life of Asa as narrated at 2 Chron. 14.8-12:

> Now Asa had an army of 300,000 from Judah... all of them were valiant warriors. Now Zerah the Ethiopian came out against them with an army of a million men and 300 chariots,

---

[1] See below Section 3c, '1 Chronicles 10: Saul'.

and he came to Mareshah. So Asa went out to meet him, and
they drew up in battle formation in the valley of Zephathah at
Mareshah. Then Asa called to Yahweh his God, and said,
'Lord, there is no one besides you to help between the powerful
and those who have no strength; so help us, O Yahweh our God,
for we trust in you and in your name have come against this
multitude. O Yahweh, you are our God; let not man prevail
against you'. So Yahweh routed the Ethiopians before Asa and
before Judah, and the Ethiopians fled.

The account continues with a narration of the plunder they
gathered.

Such examples are presented as past facts. Aristotle noted
there are two varieties of examples: one draws on actual past
events; the other relies on the invention of material in the form
of a parable or of a fable.[1] In the case of 'deliberative' or
'political' rhetoric, a category to which Chronicles is similar,[2]
examples based on actual events carry more weight, for Aristotle says, 'while it is easier to supply parallels by inventing
fables, it is more valuable for the political speaker to supply
them by quoting what has actually happened, since in most
respects the future will be like what the past has been'.[3]

2. *The Logical Structure of the Argument*
a. *Introduction to the Topoi*
Turning from the identification of the argument as demonstrated through the enthymeme and the example, one needs
to consider how the argument is constructed. Aristotle examined the construction of arguments in terms of what he called
the 'topoi'. Topoi represent the ways the mind works to gen-
eralize, classify, analyze and synthesize that which it per-
ceives.[4] Some topoi are material aids to the invention of arguments, while others are formal aids. That is, some are the
'places' where one looks for something to say about the subject

[1] Aristotle, II. 20. 1394a25-30.
[2] See Chapter 2 D, 'Type of Rhetoric'.
[3] Aristotle, II. 20. 1394a6-8.
[4] E.P. Corbett, *Classical Rhetoric for the Modern Student* (New York:
Oxford University Press, 1965), p. 108.

under discussion, while others represent the patterns one uses to express the argument.[1]

There are three types of topoi discussed by Aristotle.[2] These are: 'commonplaces' (*koina*), 'specific topics' (*eidē*), and 'common topics' (*koinoi topoi*).[3] The first two, the commonplaces and the specific topics, provide material for arguments. The commonplaces provide premises common to the three kinds of rhetoric as well as to other arts and sciences. The specific topics provide premises specific to each of the three genres of rhetoric. The third type of the topoi, the common topics, however, 'are formal methods of inference according to which enthymemes can be constructed through the use of the premises provided by the *eidē* and *koina*'.[4] Taking a look at these, briefly, we can observe and classify the topoi used by the Chronicler.

b. *Commonplaces*
The commonplaces apply to all three types of rhetoric and consist of four kinds of propositions. One can argue: (1) about whether something is possible or impossible, (2) about whether a thing has or has not occurred, (3) about whether it will or will not occur, (4) and about whether it has some property to a greater or lesser degree.[5] Little needs to be said about the Chronicler's use of the commonplaces in the invention of his argument. In his historical narrative the Chronicler has drawn on the first two commonplaces; that is, he sought to demonstrate that his argument about seeking was quite

[1] Kennedy, *New Testament Interpretation*, p. 20.
[2] Aristotle's discussion of the topoi in *Rhetoric* leaves the reader with much unclarified. As a result, the distinctions between the types of topoi are variously debated. The following description adheres to what seems to be the general consensus among Aristotelian scholars.
[3] Arnhart, p. 51.
[4] *Ibid.* Kennedy (*Persuasion*, pp. 100-103) also agrees that the topics first discussed are material, while those of II. 23 are formal.
[5] Aristotle, I. 3. 1359a-12-26. Arnhart concludes there are three kinds of propositions, combining the second and third kinds above into one category (p. 50). Aristotle does list these two kinds together in this passage, but in a later passage (II. 19) he separates his discussion of past fact from that of future fact, so that it appears he thought in terms of four kinds. Kennedy as well finds four kinds (*Persuasion*, p. 101).

clearly a possible source of action (1), and that the pattern of this principle being worked out had repeatedly occurred in the past (2). Thereby he also implied the third commonplace, that this principle continues to be efficacious in the present and the future.

c. *Special Topics*

The special topics require a greater depth of treatment. There are three special topics, each appropriate for one of the three types of rhetorical speech. As we have noted, Aristotle concluded that there are three types of rhetorical speech: deliberative, judicial and ceremonial. Deliberative speech focuses primarily on political concerns. In this type of rhetoric one desires to persuade the audience to make a decision regarding a course of action to be taken in the future. In judicial rhetoric the focus is on moving the audience to make a judgment on a past act. Ceremonial rhetoric seeks to move an audience to accept the praise or censure of someone. All three types of rhetoric may be present in a given speech, but generally one type will predominate according to the main purpose of the speech.

As already mentioned, Chronicles should be classified primarily as deliberative speech.[1] In retelling the story of Judah, the Chronicler presented the past in such a way as to counsel his audience as to what course of action should be taken by them in future. In the narrative one finds the topics of deliberative speech. However, Chronicles is not a pure example of deliberative speech, for through its depiction of the main characters and events the audience is also expected to be moved to praise and censure and to make a judgment on the past. It, therefore, also exemplifies the marks of ceremonial and judicial rhetoric and utilizes the special topics for those types of speech. The persuasive appeal of the Chronicler's argument may be further illuminated by taking a brief look at his employment of each of the three types of special topics.

---

[1] See Chapter 2 D, 'Types of Rhetoric'.

(1) *The Special Topics of Deliberative Speech*

Aristotle names five important subjects for the deliberative speaker in a political context: ways and means, war and peace, defense of the country, imports and exports, and legislation.[1] The final end for which the deliberative speaker must argue concerning these subjects is the happiness of every individual.[2] As Edward Corbett phrases it:

> When we are trying to persuade someone to do something, we try to show him that what we want him to do is either good or advantageous. All of our appeals in this kind of discourse can be reduced to these two heads: (1) the worthy (*dignitas*) or the good (*bonum*) and (2) the advantageous or expedient or useful (*utilitas*).[3]
>
> In summary then, let us say that when we are engaged in any kind of deliberative discourse, we are seeking to convince someone to adopt a certain course of action because it is conducive to his happiness or to reject a certain course of action because it will lead to unhappiness.[4]

These appeals constitute the special topics for deliberative speech. These topics provide 'material' for the Chronicler's invention/development of the argument regarding seeking. Seeking Yahweh results in blessing. And blessing has been described in Chronicles in national-political terms: a wise and wealthy Davidic king who rules justly, who engages in building projects, who raises an army and fortifies the land, whose army is victorious in war, and whose nation is ultimately granted peace by Yahweh. Seeking Yahweh results in blessing, and blessing is to be desired because it brings about what is good and advantageous for national and personal well-being. Forsaking Yahweh has also been shown to bring about results that are disadvantageous.

(2) *The Special Topics of Ceremonial Speech*

The topics of ceremonial speech are employed in the Chronicler's characterization of the kings. The special topics of ceremonial discourse are virtue and vice, the noble and the base;

---

[1] Aristotle, I. 4. 1359b19-22.
[2] *Ibid.*, I. 5. 1360B4-7.
[3] Corbett, p. 146.
[4] *Ibid.*, p. 148.

these are the objects of praise and censure.[1] To illustrate more precisely the qualities the rhetor should emphasize in order to effect praise or censure, Aristotle defined a number of virtues (e.g. justice, courage, temperance, magnificence, magnanimity, liberality, gentleness, prudence and wisdom) and their opposites.[2] Although the Chronicler depicted his heroes as possessing some of these characteristics (e.g. the wisdom of Solomon), his concept of virtue assumed a narrow scope. According to the Chronicler, one primarily exhibited virtue and nobleness by seeking Yahweh, as manifest by one's care for proper cultic procedure.

Aristotle also observed that the use of amplification and depreciation, which is essentially one of the common topics (4),[3] is quite suitable for ceremonial discourse.[4] Corbett has given a succinct list of Aristotle's ways of heightening praise, most of which can be found in Chronicles:

1. Show that a man is the first one or the only one or almost the only one to do something. (David [and Solomon] are the first to bring back the ark to Jerusalem, to build the temple, to establish the divisions in the cultic personnel, and so forth.)

2. Show that a man has done something better than anyone else, for superiority of any kind is thought to reveal excellence. (Saul was set up as a foil to which David was contrasted. David and Solomon became the standard to which the succeeding kings were compared.)

3. Show that a man has often achieved the same success, for this will indicate that his success was due not to chance but to his own powers. (David was repeatedly victorious in war. His victories were due neither to chance nor to his own powers, but, according to the Chronicler's model for success, because Yahweh aided him.)

4. Show the circumstances under which a man accomplished something, for it will redound more to his credit if he has accomplished something under adverse conditions.

---

1 Aristotle, I. 9. 1366a23-24.
2 *Ibid.*, I. 9. 1366b1-22.
3 This connection was pointed out by Corbett (p. 154).
4 Aristotle, I. 9. 1368a10-28.

(This was particularly true of the 'good' kings Hezekiah and Josiah, who succeeded wicked kings.)

5. Compare him with famous men, for the praise of a man will be magnified if we can show that he has equaled or surpassed other great men. (David surpassed Saul, the good Davidic kings are shown to have surpassed their predecessors who failed to seek Yahweh.)[1]

Aristotle realized that praising a man was similar to urging a course of action.[2] This is to say that ceremonial discourse sometimes shaded off into deliberative discourse, as it could into judicial. When praising a great man for his virtues and deeds, at least indirectly, the orator is suggesting that such would be an appropriate course of action for the audience as well.[3] To this end, Aristotle noted that the use of examples of famous men is most suitable to deliberative speeches.[4]

(3) *The Special Topics of Judicial Speech*
In judicial discourse, the over-arching special topics are those of justice and injustice.[5] After defining injustice, or 'wrongdoing', Aristotle examined three subjects which the rhetor needs to understand in order to argue in the realm of accusation and defense: the motives of wrong doing, the conditions under which one commits wrongs and the kinds of persons who are wronged.[6] These topics play little part in Chronicles. The Chronicler was much more interested in the event of violating divine laws than in the motivation behind the action. As has been pointed out in Chapter 2, the Chronicler had little interest in depicting the internal side of his characters. Rather, he painted his characters simply in broad strokes, judging their character on the basis of their cult-related actions and the consequences of those actions.

---

[1] Corbett, pp. 154-55.
[2] Aristotle, I. 9. 1367b36.
[3] Corbett, too, makes this point (p. 152).
[4] Aristotle, I. 9. 1368a29-31.
[5] Corbett, p. 150.
[6] Aristotle, I. 10. 1368b1-5. These topics are discussed in I. 10-12.

d. *Conclusion over the Material Topoi: Commonplaces and Special Topics*

The above topics provide material for stating and restating one's argument. A skilled rhetor understands the differences between a learned audience evaluating matters of science and a general audience weighing probabilities. A learned audience might be capable of hearing the proof of a thesis on one hearing and be persuaded. But, a general audience, to be persuaded, requires that the argument be repeated several times in different ways. These topics provided the material means for the Chronicler to state and restate his argument before his audience.

e. *Common Topics*
(1) *Introduction*

The topics which Aristotle lists in Book II, chs. 23–23, the 'common topics' (*koinoi topoi*), unlike the previous ones, do not provide material for arguments; rather, they are logical structures for demonstration. They provide formal methods of inference according to which enthymemes can be constructed. For example, regarding the first topic listed here, Aristotle states:

> One line of positive proof is based upon consideration of the opposite of the thing in question. Observe whether that opposite has the opposite quality. If it has not, you refute the original proposition; if it has, you establish it.[1]

A pattern for this topic would be:

> If A is the contrary of B, and C is the contrary of D, then if C is predicated of A, then D is predicated of B.[2]

One need only to fill in the variables with appropriate terms. An illustration Aristotle gives is, 'Temperance is beneficial; for licentiousness is hurtful'.[3]

---

[1] *Ibid.*, II. 23. 1397a7-10.
[2] Ryan (pp. 97-113) presents and illustrates the logical patterns of Aristotle's topics for genuine and non-genuine enthymemes found in II. 23-24.
[3] Aristotle, II. 23. 1397a10-11.

(2) *The Chronicler's Formal Topic*
In order to identify which of the topics described by Aristotle is used by the Chronicler to form the main enthymeme, it is necessary to take a closer look at the Chronicler's enthymeme regarding the death of Saul: 'Saul died and lost his kingdom, because he failed to seek Yahweh'.

The premise of the enthymeme in this argument is constituted by a maxim, a commonly accepted opinion about a generally applicable principle. The maxim is, 'Yahweh blesses those who act in the manner he prescribes and forsakes or curses those who do not'. The concept that Yahweh blessed certain types of behavior and cursed others was not a new concept. One finds the idea of divine retribution in the Samuel–Kings narrative, in legal material, in wisdom material and in the prophets; in short, throughout the Old Testament. The Chronicler built his enthymeme on a concept he could safely assume his audience accepted as a foundational truth. According to Aristotle, building an enthymeme on such generally accepted principles invests a speech with moral character and gains the audience's favor:

> There is another [advantage of using a maxim] which is more important—it invests a speech with moral character. There is moral character in every speech in which the moral purpose is conspicuous: and maxims always produce this effect, because the utterance of them amounts to a general declaration of moral principles: so that, if the maxims are sound, they display the speaker as a man of sound moral character.[1]

More significantly, the Chronicler took this general maxim of divine retribution and, in the following account of David and Solomon, he qualified it and redefined it in terms of his paradigm of seeking Yahweh. Seeking Yahweh becomes connected with the proper cultic forms of worship. Blessing takes the form of having one's kingdom established, prosperity, building projects, fortification, military success and so forth. Being forsaken by Yahweh results in the opposite. Further details about the duration of the consequences and how the consequences could be reversed are taught and illustrated in

---

[1] *Ibid.*, II. 21. 1395b12-17; see 1395b1-17.

the following narration of Israel's history, particularly in the form of examples.

In the formal topic used by the Chronicler, the maxim is related causally to a specific event by a connecting 'sign' which reveals that the principle is in effect. Saul died in battle, Saul lost his kingdom. Here is a sign that the negative corollary of this principle is in effect. The logical structure behind this kind of enthymeme may be expressed as follows:

If A is a sign of B, and A has occurred, then one can predicate B.

An enthymeme based on this structure, according to Aristotle, is non-genuine.[1] Its power to persuade is dependent upon the nature of the sign. A genuine and convincing enthymeme can be based on a 'necessary sign'. For instance, since thunder is a necessary sign of lightning, one could state, 'It thundered, because there was lightning'. Non-necessary signs, in contrast, are based on common opinion. An enthymeme built on such a sign is formally unconvincing, because one only needs to find one exception to the rule to ruin the argument.[2]

The persuasiveness of the Chronicler's enthymeme, therefore, rested upon the degree to which his audience believed the maxim and accepted the relationship between the signs and the maxim. In telling his story the Chronicler faced the danger of providing the audience with a counter-example. The accounts of David and Solomon had to be told in such a way that the relationship between the signs and the principle could not be countered. There are instances where the Chronicler had problems demonstrating the principle when it did not fit smoothly with other tradition. One instance is the example given above regarding Rehoboam. Although Rehoboam and the leaders humbled themselves, they were not completely delivered from the hand of Shishak. However, the word of Yahweh which came to Shemaiah explains that deliverance was only partial so that Judah could learn a lesson about

---

[1] See the description of the fourth non-genuine enthymeme in Aristotle (II. 24. 1401b9-13).

[2] For a fuller discussion, see Ryan (pp. 83-88).

service to Yahweh and service to other kingdoms (2 Chron. 12.6-8).

3. *The Development and Complementary Use of Enthymemes and Examples*

a. *Introduction*

The nature and style of the rhetorical presentation determines the manner in which one uses enthymemes and examples in relation to each other. Aristotle observed that when examples precede enthymemes, the argument takes on an inductive air. For such an argument to be convincing, one must give a large number of examples. On the other hand, when examples follow enthymemes they function much like the testimony of witnesses. In the latter case a single example might be sufficient, if it is a good one.[1] The question we want to turn to now is how the Chronicler used enthymemes and examples in relation to one another to present his argument effectively.

The Chronicler's narrative offered a new, or at least a reformed, interpretation of his audience's traditions; that is, he saw much of Israel's story as shaped by the principle of 'seeking'. To present such a new interpretation blatantly, using enthymemes at the beginning of a work, would increase the likelihood of its rejection, unless the speaker wielded the authority necessary to demand that the audience reject the old and accept the new. On the other hand, to present a new interpretation inductively through examples creates less of a demand on a speaker's authority. However, to offer a string of historical examples without explicit and interpretive enthymemes would increase the possibility of failing to communicate the point. One finds that the Chronicler's presentation reveals a skillful and delicately balanced employment of examples and enthymemes.

In the following analysis it will be observed that the Chronicler's demonstration through enthymemes moves: (1) from infrequent use to frequent use, (2) from being presented in unobtrusive material to more obtrusive material, and (3) from being related to traditionally accepted signs to being related to the more specific signs connected to the concept of seeking. His

---

[1] Aristotle, II. 20. 1394a9-17.

demonstration through example moves from the creation of the whole David–Solomonic paradigm, which in itself contains examples of seeking Yahweh, to a succession of examples found in the accounts of the Davidic kings.

b. *1 Chronicles 1–9*
In the genealogical lists of the first nine chapters, the argument appears proleptically five times in enthymemes. These 'argue' a maxim of divine blessing/punishment and are based on signs and relationships traditionally accepted: Judah's son, Er, was 'wicked' and put to death (2.3), certain Israelite tribes were victorious in battle because they cried out to God and trusted him (5.20, 22), exile occurred because Israel 'played the harlot' after other gods (5.25-26) and because Judah was 'unfaithful' (9.1). In the midst of various lists, such narrative comments stand out and begin to direct the thinking of the audience to the principles operative in the world.

c. *1 Chronicles 10: Saul*
Once the narrative proper begins at ch. 10, the argument is first clearly and blatantly stated in enthymematic form in connection with an example, Saul's death. It is stated 'blatantly' because it occurs in a narrative comment, that is, in material which 'breaks frame' with the action of the narrative and provides an interpretation or explanation. The Chronicler as narrator becomes most visible to his audience in such material and leaves himself and his argument open to challenge by the audience. Such blatant presentations of the enthymeme are rare in the first half of the Chronicler's work. Only twice in the following material about David and Solomon are there enthymemes about God's intervention in the form of narrative comments, and these concern the proper cultic procedure for the transportation of the ark (1 Chron. 13.10; 15.25-26), two occasions which will help to define the Chronicler's particular concept of 'seeking'. His general argument is not again demonstrated by an enthymeme in narrative-comment material until one reaches the accounts of the Davidic monarchs.[1] By then the argument has been well

---

[1] See List 1 in the Appendix.

established by the use of example and by presenting the enthymeme in other types of material.

This first enthymematic comment reveals some persuasive subtlety that should not be overlooked. As a narrative explanation it carries the risk of leaving the Chronicler as narrator open to challenge. As an enthymeme based on a sign topic, it is also open to refutation by counter-example.[1] Still, the Chronicler has minimized the risks very strategically in a couple of ways. First, because similar enthymemes occurred in the prior list material of the first nine chapters, the evaluation fits in with a train of thought already introduced, thus lessening the obtrusive impact it might have made. Secondly, the Chronicler is careful not to stray far from tradition. Virtually all of the chapter (with the exception of the unique tradition about the disposal of Saul's head [v. 10b]) through v. 13 is equivalent verbatim to the tradition of 1 Sam. 31.1-13. (We have argued that such parallel material was probably known in some form to the intended audience.) Then begins this unique narrative comment, which draws on traditional thinking. The cause of Saul's demise in the older tradition was primarily regarded as Saul's failure to obey the commands of Yahweh (1 Sam. 13.13-14; 15.23). This is what the Chronicler alludes to when he states, 'Saul died... because of the word of Yahweh which he did not keep' (v. 13). His enthymeme up to this point is persuasive for two reasons: first, it is based on a maxim that he can safely assume his audience would accept, that Yahweh rewards obedience and punishes disobedience; and, secondly, the maxim's relationship to the sign, Saul's death, is supported by the weight of older tradition. Up to this point, the Chronicler has risked nothing. He has presented himself as one in agreement with his audience. He then adds to this general reason another specific transgression of Saul's, which also belonged to older tradition: Saul also failed to obey Yahweh when he inquired of the medium at Endor, the event at which his defeat was announced (1 Sam. 28.8-19). The Chronicler, making a play on Saul's name for heightened effect, includes Saul's (שָׁאוּל) act of asking (שָׁאַל) the medium as

---

[1] See the discussion above on 'signs', under (2) 'The Chronicler's Formal Topic'.

the specific cause of Saul's death (v. 13). This conclusion, while
not stated explicitly in the Book of Samuel, would have followed by analogy. Here was another transgression of Saul and
the particular one at which his defeat was prophesied.

The Chronicler sums up the evaluation, adding a new element: 'Now he did not seek (דרשׁ) Yahweh, so he put him to
death' (v. 14). The new element is that the maxim of blessing/
punishment is connected to the action of seeking or not seeking Yahweh. Here 'seeking' occurs with the same technical
nuance found in its use in Samuel–Kings, that of prophetic
inquiry or consultation, so that its occurrence here is quite
appropriate.[1] The audience is prepared to accept that identification of 'not seeking' with 'not keeping the word of Yahweh'.
However, by the end of Chronicles 'seeking' will have been
used some thirty-five times in a much broader sense, such as:
establishing the cult (1 Chron. 28.9), keeping the torah (2
Chron. 14.3), walking in God's commandments (2 Chron.
17.4), destroying Asherahs (2 Chron. 19.3), and so on.[2] As a
result, the maxim of divine retribution becomes applied to a
new range of actions and events. In short, the Chronicler
introduced his enthymeme in a rather obtrusive form of
material while at the same time lessening the chance of rejection by building on a safe example from the tradition of the
audience. At the same time he began a program to move the
audience to accept a transformed understanding of the process of blessing/punishment by using a key term with an
accepted range of meaning, which he would later expand. As
corollary to these observations, one can presume that the
Chronicler did not view himself as having sufficient personal
authority to move his audience to accept his argument
through a more direct form of presentation.

d. *1 Chronicles 11–2 Chronicles 9: David and Solomon*
(1) *Examples*
In the account of David and Solomon, various actions of
'seeking Yahweh' which led to blessing are narrated. As has

---

[1] Throntveit, pp. 116-18. See also Schaefer (pp. 62-66) on the use of דרשׁ
in a religious context.
[2] *Ibid.*; Braun, 'Significance', pp. 172-74.

been observed in Chapter 2 on the structure of Chronicles, David and Solomon are presented typologically as ones who properly sought Yahweh and received blessing. The examples in this portion of the Chronicler's story redefine the maxim of blessing/punishment. Blessing becomes more clearly tied to the establishment and maintenance of cultic concerns. Taken as a whole this material establishes the Chronicler's major historical paradigm, according to which the actions of the succeeding Davidic kings are measured.

(2) *Enthymemes*

Only twice in the account of David and Solomon does the enthymeme occur in narrative comments (1 Chron. 13.10; 15.25-26), and these instances, related to the transportation of the ark to Jerusalem (something Saul failed to do), help to define the concept of seeking Yahweh in cultic terms. When improper cultic procedures were used, disaster followed (1 Chron. 13.10). When proper cultic procedures are heeded, success occurs (1 Chron. 15.25-26).

The enthymematic form of the argument appears thirteen more times in this section, but primarily in a particular type of material. Rather than in the more obtrusive form of a narrative evaluation it occurs in speeches of authoritative characters, Yahweh, David and Solomon.[1] The vehicle of speech material allows the Chronicler as narrator to remain in the background and yet communicate the enthymeme through the medium of authoritative characters. Therefore, the acceptance of these enthymemes rests less on the authority of the speaker of the narrative, the Chronicler, and more on the authority of the characters speaking. In these occurrences the argument becomes increasingly defined and more boldly phrased.

The first two illustrations of this subtle communication of the enthymeme are found in the section in which the Davidic dynasty is secured (1 Chron. 17). The enthymeme is communicated by implication in an expression of the reciprocal principle of 'establishing', that is, as David establishes Yahweh's

---

[1] See List 2 in the Appendix.

house, Yahweh establishes David's. Yahweh, via Nathan, promises:

> He [Solomon] will build for me a house, and I will establish (כן)
> his throne forever (v. 12).

David responds in a lengthy prayer:

> And now, Yahweh, let [your] word... concerning his house be
> established (אמן)... And let your name be *established* (אמן) and
> magnified forever, saying, 'Yahweh of hosts is the God of Israel
> ... and the house of David your servant is established (כון) before
> you (vv. 23-24).[1]

Although it is not explicitly stated, the context of events should lead one to see that David has 'sought Yahweh' by desiring to build the temple, and Yahweh has consequently blessed David by promising to found his dynasty. Thus, the application of the Chronicler's maxim is implied. Again, this expression of the maxim is based on tradition found in synoptic material (2 Sam. 7). The Chronicler chose to include in his narrative a key event/speech which would demonstrate to his audience the connection of establishing the cult to the operation of the divine law of blessing.

One finds the negative expression of divine retribution in the next two instances of the enthymeme, 1 Chron. 21.8 and 17. These instances also occur in a synoptic passage and again express the point rather implicitly in two prayers of David. Having sinned by ordering a census, David incurred punishment on himself and his people. Praying to Yahweh (i.e. an expression of seeking), David confesses his responsibility and asks that the judgment on the people be diverted, which occurs. It is possible that the Chronicler included the census event, which presents the only flaw of David, primarily because this event records how the temple site was obtained. Still, this synoptic tradition both illustrates and implicitly states the Chronicler's argument.

At the close of David's life, in two sets of parallel speeches, which bracket cultic-list material, David proclaims the enthy-

---

[1] The second occurrence of אמן in vv. 23-24 is not found in the parallel verses in 2 Sam. 7. It is possible that the Chronicler has added it to his source in order to highlight this reciprocal relationship.

meme with increasing specificity. In ch. 22, in a charge to Solomon, David repeats the promise about the reciprocal relationship of establishing and adds further:

> Now, my son, may Yahweh be with you, so that you may suc-
> ceed and build the house of Yahweh your God just as he
> promised concerning you. Only may Yahweh give you discretion
> and understanding, when he gives you command over Israel, to
> keep the law of Yahweh your God. Then you will prosper, if you
> are careful to do the statutes, and the judgments... (22.11-13).

And to the leaders he charges:

> Is not Yahweh your God with you, and has given you rest from
> all sides?... Now set your heart and your soul to seek Yahweh
> your God; and arise and build the sanctuary of Yahweh God...
> (22.18-19).

Then in the parallel speeches in ch. 28, which invert the order of those addressed, David, quoting the promise of Yahweh, first gives a charge to the leaders:

> And I will establish [כון] his kingdom forever, if he resolutely
> performs my commandments and my ordinances, as at this
> day. So now... observe and seek after all the commandments of
> Yahweh your God in order that you may possess the good
> land... (28.7-8).

And David charges Solomon, stating the enthymeme explic-itly:

> Serve Yahweh with a whole heart. If you seek him, he will let
> you find him; but if you forsake him, he will reject you forever
> (28.9b).

Some observations should be made regarding the use of the enthymeme in the above passages. These speeches are unique to Chronicles. It is possible that the Chronicler has gone beyond the range of tradition known to his audience. If so, the risk of the argument being rejected is again reduced by the type of material used to convey it. The type of material in which the enthymeme is presented is not obtrusive narrative comments, but speeches by an authoritative person, speeches which are 'in character' for the Chronicler's presentation of David. At the same time there is a special force to the point made, because it is in the format of a speech. Not only does the king address the narrative audience, but also the actual audience of the Chronicler is likely to feel the force of the direct address. As David speaks to Solomon and the Israelite leaders, the Chronicler speaks to his audience. The fact that in these two sets of speeches the content is basically the same and the order of those addressed is inverted (i.e. Solomon–leaders–leaders–Solomon) calls attention to the fact that the sets of speeches form an *inclusio*. They bracket material consisting primarily of lists of cultic personnel appointed by David and, therefore, further demonstrate his vital role in establishing the temple cultus (see 1 Chron. 23.5a, 6, 25-27; 24.3, 31; 25.1, 6; 26.[26], 30-32).[1]

The 'causal' relationship of blessing to seeking Yahweh with one's heart through observing proper cultic practice is more clearly argued in these speeches. In the account of Solomon, the same pattern is followed. The events chosen by the Chronicler give examples of Solomon seeking Yahweh and receiving blessing in return. The enthymematic clarification of this relationship is stated directly only in speech material found in the mouths of Yahweh and Solomon. By the end of the account of David and Solomon the causal relationship of seeking Yahweh to blessing has been forcefully argued.

e. *2 Chronicles 10–36: The Davidic Kings*
Once the Chronicler's argument had been established in the Davidic-Solomonic paradigm, the events in the following lives of the Davidic kings further exemplified the Chronicler's fuller maxim of blessing/punishment which he saw at work in the nation's history.[2] The enthymeme occurs more frequently and in more blatant form in this part of the Chronicler's story. There, it is stated twenty-three times in speech material, and twenty times in the more obtrusive form of narrative-explanatory comments.[3]

---

[1] Chapters 23–26 consist of personnel who did service either for the temple or for the temple and the king (26.29-32), while ch. 27 consists of personnel who served just the king.
[2] See Chapter 2, section C 2c, '1 Chronicles 10–2 Chronicles 9: The Davidic and Solomonic Paradigm'.
[3] See Lists 1 and 2 in the Appendix.

Summary and Conclusion

The Chronicler used a supportive balance of demonstration by
enthymeme and example. His thesis is first stated by an
example with an accompanying enthymeme in a 'high-risk'
form of narrative comment regarding the death of Saul. The
Chronicler decreased the risk by basing what he said on an
appeal to tradition and a common understanding of the divine
principle of blessing/punishment. This principle is then both
expanded to include a broader range of actions and supported
inductively by the lives of David and Solomon. In this material
the enthymeme is infrequently stated, and then only in
speeches by authoritative characters. The accounts of the succeeding kings are structured so as to serve as a series of
examples showing the results of seeking or forsaking Yahweh.
Among these examples, the Chronicler proceeded with
greater boldness. The enthymeme is more frequently stated,
primarily still in the speeches of authoritative characters, but
now in the form of narrative comments. That is to say, the
author moved from a primarily inductive and safe presentation of his argument to a presentation that used examples as
'witnesses' to support more frequent declarative/explanatory
statements of the argument. The Chronicler moved from
making his case subtly and cautiously to stating it more openly
and forcefully once he felt it had been sufficiently established.

As has been remarked, a good communicator knows that in
the demonstration of an argument to a general audience one
must present an argument in an appealing manner and must
repeat the basic idea several times in different ways. The
Chronicler did that. Through his presentation of the story of
Judah, he implicitly was saying:

> As you know, there is a principle operating in this world, a
> principle according to which Yahweh blesses or curses. Bless-
> ing is contingent upon seeking Yahweh through establishing
> and maintaining the cult of Yahweh. Surely you will want to
> take this course of action of seeking Yahweh, because it results
> in what is good and advantageous for you. Surely you will want
> to do this because it is virtuous. See the examples from your
> past, make the comparisons, and judge for yourselves. Look at
> David and Solomon. They sought Yahweh and were blessed.
> Look at those who were without such virtue. You certainly do

not desire for yourselves what happened to them. What course, then, will you choose?

In conclusion, the Chronicler has made an artful and persuasive appeal on the rational level of his work.

Chapter 4

ETHOS: THE ETHICAL MODE OF PERSUASION

A. Introduction

1. *Aristotle's Criteria*

The purpose of this chapter is to describe the ethical mode of persuasion in the books of Chronicles. Every rhetor 'invents' a strategy for communicating his/her message in such a way that the audience, hopefully, will be persuaded to receive the message and act on it. As has been noted, a key component of this strategy are the three modes of persuasion or artistic proofs: logos, the appeal of the speech as it demonstrates rationally; ethos, the ethical appeal; and, pathos, the emotional appeal made to the audience. The ethical appeal is based on the communication of the character of the rhetor through the speech. Good rhetors present themselves as credible and worthy of trust.

According to Aristotle, the ethical appeal was in a practical sense the most effective or authoritative means of persuasion.

> Persuasion is achieved by the speaker's personal character when the speech is so spoken as to make us think him credible. We believe good men more fully and more readily than others: this is true generally whatever the question is, and absolutely true where exact certainty is impossible and opinions are divided. This kind of persuasion, like the others, should be achieved by what the speaker says, not by what people think of his character before he begins to speak. It is not true, as some writers assume in their treatises on rhetoric, that the personal goodness revealed by the speaker contributes nothing to his power or persuasion; on the contrary, his character may almost be called the most effective means of persuasion he possesses.[1]

---

[1] Aristotle, I. 2. 1356a.

The need for the speaker to appear as trustworthy was particularly important in political speaking, whereas an appeal to the audience's emotion was more important for lawsuits.[1]

What is it that makes a speaker's character appear trustworthy in the eyes of an audience? Aristotle named three features:

> There are three things which inspire confidence in the orator's own character—the three, namely, that induce us to believe a thing apart from any proof of it: good sense, good moral character, and goodwill. False statements and bad advice are due to one or more of the following three causes. Men either form a false opinion through want of good sense; or they form a true opinion, but because of their moral badness do not say what they really think; or finally, they are both sensible and upright, but not well disposed to their hearers, and may fail in consequence to recommend what they know to be the best course. These are the only possible cases. It follows that any one who is thought to have all three of these good qualities will inspire trust in his audience.[2]

The first attribute mentioned by Aristotle, 'good sense', is defined as, 'that virtue of the understanding which enables men to come to wise decisions about the relation to happiness of the goods and evils that have previously been mentioned'.[3] One can infer from this definition that the speaker's good sense can be evaluated by judging the soundness of the speech.[4] Does the speaker reveal a good understanding of that about which he or she is speaking? Are the arguments appropriate? Are the enthymemes logically sound? Are they popularly accepted? Are they accepted by others who are recognized as prudent? Do the examples show a thorough knowledge of the data? Are the examples truly analogous to the point being argued? In other words, does the speaker demonstrate an understanding of the relation between the decision the hearers are to make and the resultant 'good' for their behalf?

---

[1] *Ibid.*
[2] *Ibid.*, II. 1. 1378a.
[3] *Ibid.*, I. 9. 1366a20-22.
[4] Arnhart, p. 113.

A speaker who lacks good sense is not likely to offer good advice.[1]

The second attribute, 'good moral character' (also called 'virtue'), is a broadly defined attribute.

> Virtue is, according to the usual view, a faculty of providing and preserving good things; or a faculty of conferring many great benefits of all kinds on all occasions. The forms of virtue are justice, courage, temperance, magnificence, magnanimity, liberality, gentleness, prudence, wisdom.[2]

A person possessing good moral character can be trusted to want the best for her/his audience. Such a person will present an argument which, if accepted, will work for the good of the audience. However, if one lacks good moral character, that person cannot be trusted to deliver even good advice sincerely.[3]

Establishing 'good will', the quality of being well disposed to one's hearers, is connected with 'friendship' and is treated under Aristotle's discussion of the emotions of friendship and enmity in Book II, chapter 4.[4] He defined 'friendly feeling' thus:

> We may describe friendly feeling towards any one as wishing for him what you believe to be good things, not for your own sake but for his, and being inclined, so far as you can, to bring these things about.[5]

The speaker who possesses 'good will' will not mislead the hearers, but will establish a disposition of friendship with the audience.

2. *Tentative Conclusions*

How does one evaluate this ethical appeal? We have no record of the audience's perception of the Chronicler, except for the fact that the work was preserved and valued by the community of faith. We have only the text through which the appeal was made. Not only must we seek to assess in the work the exhibition of Aristotle's attributes (good sense, good moral

---

1 *Ibid.*, p. 112.
2 Aristotle, I. 9. 1366a-1366b.
3 Arnhart, pp. 112-13.
4 Aristotle, II. 1. 1378a19.
5 *Ibid.*, II. 4. 1380b35-1381a1.

character, and good will), but also we must attempt to recover
to some degree the speaker's perceived audience and the likely
responses of the actual audience. Granted that these tasks call
for some speculation, some general observations can be made,
from which some tentative conclusions may be drawn.

On the general level of style, Michael Fishbane has noticed
that the Chronicler spoke with the authoritative voice of the
historian; that is, the narrative voice is omniscient and, for the
most part, unobtrusive.[1] The Chronicler displayed his knowledge of Israel's past, but avoided first-person references.[2] As a
result, 'the reader is confronted with *the* account of the past,
and not with a vision of the events or a polemical rebuttal of
other viewpoints'.[3] That which the audience received was presented by the Chronicler as authoritative tradition.

In addition, a good speaker must display more than a
knowledge of certain events. In order to exhibit the first of
Aristotle's attributes, 'good sense', the rhetor must perceive a
'correct' or acceptable relationship between these events in
order to offer sound advice. For the Chronicler's explanation
of the enthymematic relationships between events to have
been even tentatively acceptable, his audience would have had
to be willing to consider their past in terms of such an ideology.
As has been observed in Chapter 3 on the rational mode of persuasion, the Chronicler appears to have been in control of the
data and to have presented arguments which were consistent
fundamentally with the Israelite world-view as expressed in
Samuel–Kings. In both accounts Yahweh is active in the historical dimension; he curses those engaged in sin; he blesses
those engaged in righteousness. Those basics are constant,
even if the Chronicler did seek a theological explanation for
historical events more frequently and openly than the edi-
tors/authors of Samuel–Kings. Although the Chronicler began
closely aligned with a traditional view of divine retribution, he
subtly redefined some of the parameters of the tradition, as has

[1] Fishbane, p. 382.
[2] As with Greek historiography, it appears that in the Old Testament
third-person narration was the standard expected. See Scholes and
Kellogg who record that in early Greek historical narratives the use of
first person was avoided, whereas it was employed in fiction (p. 243).
[3] Fishbane, p. 382.

been observed. Modifications entered into the story-line primarily at two points: (1) on a level of definition, the Chronicler's concept of 'sinful' and 'righteous' activities is identified in terms of seeking Yahweh through proper cultic means; (2) in regard to the duration of retribution, the Chronicler perceived a repeated pattern of reversal between cursing and blessing in the story of Israel. Even with these modifications, one might suppose that the post-exilic community, which had experienced the reversal from curse to blessing and whose community life increasingly was focused on the cult, would at least have been open to hearing the Chronicler's account with its particular enthymemes and implicit advice. In general one can conclude that the Chronicler was perceived by the audience as exhibiting good sense.

To some degree, the Chronicler's moral character and disposition toward the audience can be evaluated by the intentions he communicated. As noted in Chapter 3, the Chronicler sought a response which was for the benefit of Israel. The advice which was implicit in his enthymemes and story-line, if taken, was meant to result in preservation and blessing for Israel. One can conclude that he exhibited intentions appropriate to one with a good moral character. Further, the tone of the work as it reveals something of the narrator's attitude does not appear to be one which would provoke rejection. It is not angry toward the audience, or sarcastic or condescending. Rather, as will be expanded on below, the tone is 'objective' and authoritative. One would suppose that the Chronicler projected a good disposition toward the listeners and probably effected a good disposition from them.

3. *Method for Further Analysis*
The above observations regarding the Chronicler's 'good sense' and 'virtue' suggest that the Chronicler would have made a fairly positive 'ethical' impact on his audience. A deeper analysis needs to be conducted, however, to uncover other features which might have influenced his audience to be well disposed toward him (i.e. to establish 'good will') and to grant him the authority to retell their history. I propose that the ethical appeal of the Chronicler is further disclosed in the

types of material with which he chose to compose his story and in the particular manner in which he utilized this material.

Approximately one-half of the Chronicler's history is set forth with material with which, we can fairly safely assume, the audience would have had some familiarity. This material in varying degrees of similarity is parallel to Samuel–Kings. The other half constitutes material which is unique to Chronicles (about 834 verses).[1] Of that material, about half consists of statistical material in the form of genealogies and lists (447 verses), a little less than half is made up of speeches (197 verses) and their narrative framework (100 verses), the remainder is additional narrative material (90 verses). Our inquiry regarding the Chronicler's use of this material will be directed according to the following lines of thought:

1. How did the Chronicler handle traditional material? If the audience was familiar with the main content and sequence of the material, then the presence and character of the rhetor would be communicated to the audience by the way the rhetor retold and reshaped those traditions. One can imagine that if the Chronicler flagrantly contradicted significant traditions, neither he nor his story would have been well received.

2. Much of the Chronicler's unique material (lists, genealogies, and, to some degree, speeches) functions similarly to what Aristotle called 'external proofs'. That is, on the surface, these materials are not presented as the Chronicler's own creative wording, resting on his authority; they are presented as external records, carrying their own authority, brought into the speech as outside evidence.[2] It is important then to note how the Chronicler used this material to further his argument.

3. Narrative material may be classified as 'straight' (primarily presents a sequence of actions), 'scenic' (depicts setting), 'descriptive' (describes the nature of the characters), or 'commentative' (comments on a feature in the account). Commentative narative interupts the flow of story to some degree. For example, some narrative comments simply serve

---

[1] This statistic and the following are taken from Rigsby (p. 70 n. 107).
[2] Aristotle, I. 2. 1355b36-40 and I. 15.

to clarify a detail or to answer a question the audience might have or in some way set the stage so that the story can once more flow on smoothly for the audience. Other comments more forcefully stop the story and give an evaluation of a character or explain a relationship between events that is not readily apparent in the presentation. The narrator's presence is particularly felt in such cases, since the presentation shifts from 'facts' to 'opinion'. And, the weight of the opinion rests on the character (ethos) of the narrator. Therefore, it will be illuminating to note how the Chronicler used explanatory comments.

B. *Analysis*

1. *Material Parallel to Samuel–Kings: Traditional Material*
a. *Methodological Assumptions*
The Chronicler was faced with a problem requiring a rhetorical strategy: how to re-present material with which his audience would be familiar, in such a way as to demonstrate his argument, and with such rhetorical skill that his retelling of their story would be accepted by his audience. Therefore, we wish to gain some insight into how the Chronicler handled the material he received, and, more importantly, how the audience would have perceived and reacted to his re-presentation of their traditional stories. Our only point of control over the historical traditions with which the Chronicler might have expected his audience to be familiar comes from the canonical books of Samuel–Kings. Approximately one-half of Chronicles consists of material parallel to material found in Samuel–Kings, some of it virtually verbatim and some of it only roughly parallel. It is not the purpose of this analysis to present a synoptic comparison of that parallel material. Such work has been done. Then, too, that work often has examined minute differences which likely would be observed only by one making a detailed literary analysis and not by an aural audience. In contrast, it is a working assumption of this book that the Chronicler expected his audience to be familiar in general with such traditions found in Samuel–Kings, but that he did not expect or desire from them a detailed, synoptic reading of

the two histories.[1] Our task is to suppose what the perceptions and reactions of the Chronicler's post-exilic community might have been. To this end, some general suggestions will be offered.

b. *Evaluation of the Chronicler's Use of Tradition*

Thomas Willi, who believes that the Chronicler had no significant extra-canonical sources, has argued that all of Chronicles can be explained as an interpretation of the Deuteronomistic History.[2] According to him, the Chronicler sought not to replace or supplement the older history, but to interpret it for his audience.[3] Although this writer believes it would be misleading to read Chronicles as merely a commentary on Samuel–Kings,[4] it is important to note, in agreement with Willi, that the Chronicler did not offer a contradictory account to his audience. This is to say, the audience was not faced with a choice between two incompatible accounts of which one was to be accepted and the other discarded. To be sure, there exist contradictions between details in the two versions, but, as Willi sought to demonstrate, these occurred as the Chronicler attempted to follow his *Vorlage*, while interpreting and reconciling it according to his post-exilic perspective.[5] The Chronicler did not seek to demonstrate that the earlier traditions were wrong.

Brevard Childs, approaching his evaluation of Chronicles from a different perspective, offers an observation which is compatible with Willi's conclusions:

> Perhaps the crucial discovery of the modern study of Chronicles is the extent to which the Chronicler sought to interpret Israel's history in relation to a body of authoritative scripture... Indeed most of the crucial exegetical moves which comprise the Chronicler's method [of historical exegesis] derive directly from his

---

[1] See Chapter 1, Section C 5, 'Reading Chronicles with Regard to Samuel–Kings'.
[2] Willi, *Die Chronik als Auslegung*.
[3] *Ibid.*, pp. 48-66.
[4] See Chapter 1, Section C 5, 'Reading Chronicles with Regard to Samuel–Kings'.
[5] Willi, pp. 59-63.

sion. Approximately one-half of the story is constituted by material unique to Chronicles. One would suppose that the issue of credibility would most likely be raised by the audience over this material, if it was new to them. Unless the Chronicler was already known and accepted by the audience as an unimpeachable authority and he knew that he could rely on this evaluation, he would be expected to tread carefully on this new ground. From the outset, it appears that he has. Approximately eight-ninths of this unique material has the nature of what Aristotle called 'external proof'. External or 'inartistic' proof is material not supposedly created by the rhetor, but brought in from an external source and used in support of the rhetor's argument. It might take the form of eye-witness testimony, physical evidence, letters, maps, etc. This kind of material carries its own authority with it. In the Chronicler's case, this external material brought in to support the argument consists of genealogies and various lists, as well as the direct quotation of speeches along with their narrative framework. Included in this appeal to outside authority is the Chronicler's citation of sources for his narrative. Technically, external proofs should be regarded separately from the internal or artistic proof of ethos. However, the incorporation of external proofs and the manner in which they are utilized do reflect a rhetor's strategy for creating an ethical appeal.

b. *Lists and Genealogies*

Of the material which from our perspective is unique to Chronicles, over half consists of statistical material of genealogies and lists.[1] Whether or not the modern critic thinks these genealogies and lists were created by the Chronicler, if the audience accepted them as genuine, then they would have regarded them as objective and authoritative in their own right. Their value as authoritative material would not depend on the assessment of the reliability of the Chronicler. Indeed, the reverse relationship would be effected. The use of 'objective' material would demonstrate the storyteller's effort to be

---

[1] Rigsby, p. 70 n. 107. These lists and genealogies are found in 1 Chron. 1–9; 12.1-22; 13.1–16.6; 23–27; 2 Chron. 17.7; 23.1; 28.12; 29.12-14; 31.11-19; 34.12; 35.8-9, 15.

reliable. The more objective material the Chronicler used in relation to new or reformed narrative tradition, the less suspect he would be. Since the unique material of Chronicles contains such a preponderance of external proofs, which would have been afforded a high degree of reliability, so, too, the Chronicler would have been highly regarded as well.

Being credited with drawing on objective records is not the only benefit the Chronicler would have gained by using these genealogies and lists. A skillful rhetor can utilize such material unobtrusively to further the argument. On the one hand, the Chronicler stands behind such material; his person is not out front to be questioned. Yet, while using such non-narrative materials, the Chronicler, as was observed in Chapter 2, effectively introduced the parameters of his story, highlighted his main themes, and conveyed the principle of his primary enthymeme. All of this was accomplished while maintaining an aura of objectivity and reliability.

c. *Citation of Sources*

The objective, authoritative tone of the Chronicler's work is also heightened by his citation of sources. Some of these citations occur in some of the genealogical lists and might be authentic.[1] Others occur in the conclusions of the narratives on the Davidic kings and differ from those cited in Samuel–Kings. These citations attribute the traditions found here to the writings of prophets and to royal court records.[2] Such references carry the weight of external witnesses; that is, they point to documentary evidence that exists external to the Chronicler's story. They transfer the burden of the reliability of the

[1] Ralph Klein ('Historical Allusions within the Genealogies of 1 Chronicles 1–9') has analyzed the brief historical narratives and allusions that occur within the genealogies. These anecdotes give data which supplement, complement, and in one case even contradict the canonical picture of Israelite history.

[2] 1 Chron. 29.29; 2 Chron. 9.29; 12.15; 13.22; 20.34; 26.22; 32.32; 33.18-19 (reading 'seers' with LXX). These citations are unique to Chronicles. Note also that 2 Chron. 24.27 mentions as the source for the acts of Joash the 'Book of Kings', a source which itself contained prophetic sources (2 Chron. 20.34; 32.32). Indeed, it should be remembered that later Judaism believed that the historical books of Joshua–Kings were books of the prophets.

account from the shoulders of the Chronicler to the sources. Again, the issue is not whether such sources actually existed or not. What is important to note is that the Chronicler utilized the ethos, the authority, inherent in the citation of such sources. And the sources in this case bear the ethos of prophetic authority. Incidentally, therefore, one must conclude that the Chronicler believed his intended audience would accept the existence of and reliability of these prophetic sources. If the audience believed in the existence of such documents, the Chronicler's credibility would be so much the more increased in their eyes.

d. *Direct Speech*
(1) *Introduction*

The lists and genealogies comprise over half of the material unique to Chronicles. Of the remaining unique material, over three-fourths is devoted to the presentation of speech material.[1] The quotation of direct speech, a major part of the Chronicler's creative strategy of composition, has the character of external proof, because it purports to be not the words of the Chronicler but the 'testimony' of other persons. Since the speeches in Chronicles are delivered by authoritative characters, it is their ethos and not the Chronicler's that gives weight to the contents of the speeches. Still, the Chronicler speaks through the material he utilized. The use of such speech material allowed the Chronicler to avoid a blatant presentation of himself and a reliance on his own authority, while allowing him to stand behind the speeches and speak through them.

In the following analysis a distinction sometimes will be made between dialogues, where there is a statement and response among two or more characters in a scene, and 'isolated' direct speech. In the latter category, when analyzing royal speech material, a further distinction will be made between 'speeches' and 'statements'. 'Statements' will refer to

---

[1] According to Rigsby (pp. 69-70), 834 verses are unique to Chronicles; 447 of these verses give statistical kinds of data; 197 verses of the remaining 387 verses of narrative are speech material; and another 100 provide the immediate context for the speeches.

brief comments which usually state a simple command or declaration of intent on behalf of the speaker. The speech material labeled 'speeches' consists of more than one sentence and/or serves a greater function of instructing others or making a case on behalf of the speaker.

(2) *Issue of Authenticity and Authority*

Both the amount of unique speech material in Chronicles and the fact that much of the speech material is uniform in style and supports the *Tendenz* of the book has given rise to questions about its authenticity.[1] In dealing with the issue of authenticity, one must try to distance oneself from the standards of the modern western world in which verbatim recording is so easily achieved and in which verbatim citation is not only expected, but also demanded by law in some contexts. One must seek to identify with the ancient world of the Near East. In the ancient Near East literary accuracy in some situations was obtainable. A variety of types of material were committed to writing very early on in Egypt and Mesopotamia. Historical material in these areas took the form of annalistic records. Inscriptions purporting to be the words of kings spoken on various occasions exist. The Assyrians even recorded synchronistic chronicles noting parallel events in other countries.[2] Colophonic material in some of the ancient Near Eastern texts attests to a scribal practice of accurately

---

[1] The uniformity of the content of the various speeches has long been observed. For a debate over their authenticity, see S.R. Driver, 'The Speeches in Chronicles', *The Expositor*, 5th ser. 1 (1895), pp. 241-56 and 2 (1895), pp. 286-308; and V. French, 'The Speeches in Chronicles: A Reply', *The Expositor*, 5th ser. 2 (1895), pp. 140-52. The nature and uniformity of some of the speeches proper prompted G. von Rad ('The Levitical Sermon in I and II Chronicles', *The Problem of the Hexateuch and Other Essays* [New York: McGraw-Hill, 1966], pp. 167-80) to label them formally as Levitical sermons, similar to the sermonic style found in Deuteronomy. Welch (pp. 42-54) thought the unique speeches of the prophets to be so stereotypical that the prophets became colorless mouthpieces for the same message. Rigsby (p. 246), in his dissertation, also concluded that the speeches in Chronicles are in the vocabulary, idiom, and syntax of the Chronicler.

[2] For a synopsis of historiography in the ancient Near East, see Rigsby (pp. 43-49); and, for a fuller treatment, see Van Seters.

copying documents from one generation to the next. Theoretically, then, some of the speeches in Chronicles could have been preserved in written or oral sources used by the Chronicler.[1] Particularly plausible would have been the preservation of royal or prophetic speeches made on public occasions. However, while this possibility needs to be borne in mind, the uniformity of the content and function of the speech material does reveal great freedom in composition on the part of the storyteller. But the issue of authenticity in the ancient world, particularly as it related to authority, was not simply a matter of whether the material was 'created' or not, although knowledge of the answer to this question might bring the issue to an end for many modern readers. Rather, the issue of authenticity was tied to the demands and expectations of the ancient audience.

Among the Greeks the creation of speeches was a standard practice of historiography. Besides simply furthering the action, speeches often functioned to give some insight into the character of the speaker or into the meaing of the historical moment of concern.[2] The creation of speeches was practiced in the rhetorical schools. There, the exercise of prosopopoeia was the practice of writing speeches for some mythological or historical personage in which his or her feelings and character were expressed.[3] Although such great freedom in function was allowed, certain conventional constraints were placed on the Greek writers of history. Speeches were expected to con-

---

[1] Claus Westermann (*Basic Forms of Prophetic Speech* [trans. H.C. White; London: Lutterworth, 1967], pp. 163-68) defended some degree of preservation of older tradition in the prophetic speeches on the basis of form and function. He found three old forms of prophetic speech in Chronicles and identified an original kernel in some of these speeches. Like the 'Judgment to the individual' prophetic speeches, all but one of these speeches were addressed to kings. He concluded that the evidence was sufficient to support a tradition that prophets were present in the Southern Kingdom throughout its history and to dispel a common contention that the Chronicler invented these prophets.

[2] M. Dibelius, 'The Speeches in Acts and Ancient Historiography', *Studies in the Acts of the Apostles* (ed. H. Greeven; trans. M. Ling; New York: Scribner's, 1956), pp. 138-85, esp. pp. 138-45; Rigsby, pp. 66-68; Van Seters, p. 37.

[3] Kennedy, *New Testament Interpretation*, pp. 23, 107.

vey the mind and character of the speaker accurately. The content was expected to be trustworthy in the sense that it had to be consistent with the character of the speaker in the given setting; that is, what he or she probably said or would have said. Thucydides commented about his method:

> With reference to the speeches in this history, some were delivered before the war began, others while it was going on; some I heard myself, others I got from various quarters; it was in all cases difficult to carry them word for word in one's memory, so my habit has been to make the speakers say what was in my opinion demanded of them by the various occasions, of course adhering as closely as possible to the general sense of what they really said.[1]

Given this qualification it was possible for speeches to be accepted as both created and 'authentic'. Whether or not creating speeches was a standard practice of Hebrew historiography, one would expect that a speech would still have to conform generally to the audience's perception of its speaker. This appears to have been a constraint upon the Chronicler as well. For example, one could not put in the mouth of David words totally contrary to the traditions about him and expect an audience to accept the account as trustworthy. Indeed, there is nothing David says in Chronicles that is out of character when compared to the tradition in Samuel–Kings. The portrayal is biased, to be sure, as has often been pointed out, but the differences are of the nature of omissions and interpolations, not contradiction. For example, David, whose heartfelt desire was to build a temple for Yahweh (2 Sam. 7 and 1 Chron. 17), becomes David who spoke of his many preparations for the building of the temple (1 Chron. 22; 28–29).[2]

---

[1] Thucydides, *The History of the Peloponnesian War* (trans. R. Crawley; rev. R. Feetham; *Great Books of the Western World*, ed. R.M. Hutchins, vol. 6; London: William Benton for Encyclopaedia Britannica, 1952), I.22.

[2] Soares (pp. 265-67) pointed out that the Chronicler's portrayal of David's connection with temple concerns, however mistaken, was nonetheless in keeping with the given traditions about David.

(3) *Function of Speeches in Relationship to the Enthymeme*
There are some noteworthy characteristics of the Chronicler's use of direct speech. One of the first observations a synoptic reader will make is that the narrative style of Samuel–Kings makes heavier use of scenes with dialogue in contrast to what is found in Chronicles.[1] Where dialogue scenes occur in Chronicles, the material is usually synoptic (1 Chron. 14.10; 17.1-2; 21.2-3, 11-13; 22–24; 2 Chron. 1.7-12; 10.4-16; 18.3-33; 25.17-18). But where the Chronicler has unique speech material, it is rarely in the form of a dialogue. Such a unique dialogue occurs only twice, in exchanges between a prophet and a king (2 Chron. 25.7-9 and 15-16). The bulk of the unique speech-material occurs in the form of isolated statements and speeches. In terms of rhetorical impact, direct speech in the forms of isolated statements and speeches can better serve as a vehicle for addressing the rhetor's audience than can dialogue. Scenes of dialogue are useful for revealing the thoughts and character of the speakers internal to the narrative, but, because of their descriptive nature, they tend to leave the actual audience on the outside observing the action. However, when one character is making a speech or statement, particularly when it is directed to a rather vague or sometimes even unspecified audience, the force of direct address to the narrator's audience is heightened. The actual, external audience can more easily enter into the narrative world and identify with the hearers. This is to say, then, that speeches can serve as a means for the rhetor to speak through the narrative speaker in order to address the rhetor's audience.

(a) *Enthymematic speech material.*[2] In his analysis of the synoptic speeches and prayers in Chronicles, Rigsby observed that some speeches were used by the Chronicler identically in their content and function to their usage in Samuel–Kings. These speeches either just furthered the narrative or, in their present form, expressed similar religious concerns.[3] However,

---

[1] Throntveit also made this observation (p. 12).

[2] See List 2 in the Appendix.

[3] Rigsby, pp. 80-141. These parallel speeches are: (1) those that further the narrative: 1 Chron. 10.1-14 and 1 Sam. 31.1-13, 1 Chron. 11.4-9 and 2 Sam. 5.6-10, 1 Chron. 11.15-19 and 2 Sam. 23.13-17, 1 Chron. 19.1-15 and 2 Sam. 10.1-14, 2 Chron. 9.1-12 and 1 Kgs 10.1-13; and, (2) religious

others speeches were 'transformed' in Chronicles so that, while their content is virtually identical, their function is different. In these later cases, the speeches in the Deuteronomic History, which focus more on political and military concerns, are more overtly connected in Chronicles to cultic and theological concerns.[1] Much of the direct-speech material in Chronicles either explicitly or implicitly states the key enthymeme. This point can be supported by looking at the data statistically. There are 107 incidences of direct speech in Chronicles.[2] Thirty-seven of these state the enthymeme. Of the enthymematic statements, twenty-eight are unique to Chronicles and nine are synoptic. Of the remaining seventy occasions of direct speech which do not state the enthymeme, thirty-seven are unique and thirty-three are synoptic. Therefore, thirty-five percent (37 out of 107) of the incidences of direct speech in Chronicles express the enthymeme. Significantly, many of these speeches are unique. The per-

---

speeches: 1 Chron. 13.5-14 and 2 Sam. 6.1-11, 1 Chron. 14.10-17 and 2 Sam. 5.19-25, 1 Chron. 17.1-27 and 2 Sam. 7.1-29, 1 Chron. 21.1-27 and 2 Sam. 24.1-25, 2 Chron. 1.7-13 and 1 Kgs 3.5-15, 2 Chron. 6.1-39 and 1 Kgs 8.12-53, 2 Chron. 7.11-22 and 1 Kgs 9.1-9, 2 Chron. 24.4-6 and 2 Kgs 12.4-7, 2 Chron. 25.4 and 2 Kgs 14.6, 2 Chron. 33.2-9 and 2 Kgs 21.2-9, 2 Chron. 34.14-28 and 2 Kgs 22.8-20. Rigsby (p. 140) concluded further in regard to the synoptic, religious speeches that the material in Samuel–Kings actually exhibits the so-called 'Chronistic *Tendenz*' to a greater degree than the parallel texts in Chronicles.

1 Rigsby, pp. 142-82. These speeches are: 1 Chron. 11.1-3 and 2 Sam. 5.1-3, 2 Chron. 2.1-12 and 1 Kgs 5.1-12, 2 Chron. 10.1-11.4 and 1 Kgs 12.1-24, 2 Chron. 16.1-6 and 1 Kgs 15.17-22, 2 Chron. 18.1-34 and 1 Kgs 22.1-40, 2 Chron. 23.1-15 and 2 Kgs 11.4-16, 2 Chron. 25.17-24 and 2 Kgs 14.8-14, 2 Chron. 32.9-17 and 2 Kgs 18.17-25 plus 19.9-13.

2 See Lists 2 and 3 in the Appendix. The reckoning of the following statistical data is dependent somewhat on subjective factors. For instance, multiple statements occurring together in a scene of dialogue have been recorded under one entry rather than each separately. Also, the reckoning of what constitutes unique speech material will vary from one analysis to another, for there are some cases where unique statements or statements with some unique elements occur in parallel material. Generally, statements in parallel tradition have been counted as unique when the whole statement and not just some detail in it is unique. For an example of a different reckoning, see Schaefer (pp. 28-29), who comes up with a total of 165 speeches with ninety-five considered parallel to Samuel–Kings.

centage of unique enthymematic speeches (43%, 28 out of 65) is more than double the percentage of synoptic enthymematic speeches (21%, 9 out of 42). Or, from another perspective, one discovers that seventy-six percent (28 out of 37) of the enthymematic speeches are unique to Chronicles. This is to say that the material the Chronicler relied on heavily in order to communicate the enthymeme through direct speech is unique to the biblical traditions which have come down to us. This material, whatever its origin, plays a major role in communicating the Chronicler's argument. In whatever manner the enthymematic statements function internally to the story (e.g. as a prophetic rebuke checking an idolatrous action of a king), they also had a rhetorical function of inculcating the Chronicler's argument in the mind of the audience.

(b) *Non-enthymematic speech material.*[1] Speech material that does not explicitly present or imply the enthymeme (70 out of 107 cases), still frequently plays a major role in communicating the Chronicler's argument by helping to develop the stereotypical portrayal of the main characters. (For the purpose of a rudimentary statistical analysis, some of these non-enthymematic speeches have been identified as either 'positive' or 'negative' according to their contribution to this function.) Many statements paint a positive portrayal of one of the narrative's characters—that is to say, positive according to the Chronicler's standards. These people, generally kings, show a concern about cultic matters: they seek Yahweh before battle, they repent and humble themselves, they restore cultic practices, etc. This material sets these people up as ones who then deserve Yahweh's favor in accord with the enthymeme. Included in this category are statements by one character who praises another (e.g. 2 Chron. 9.5-8). On the other hand, there are negative statements that portray a character deserving of rebuke and judgment. Finally, there are those statements which are rather neutral in terms of presenting or re-enforcing the Chronicler's themes. Certainly they have a function internal to the narrative, often simply to move the story along or to explain a certain element, but they contribute little to the argument.

[1] See List 3 in the Appendix.

Of these seventy non-enthymematic cases four demonstrate a negative character, and forty present a positive characterization. Of the forty positive cases, twenty-three are unique to Chronicles. Further, the bulk of the positive statements are found in the Davidic–Solomonic period. During the Davidic–Solomonic period one finds twenty-seven positive statements and one negative, whereas in the presentations of the following Davidic kings there are thirteen positive and three negative statements.

(c) *Distribution of non-enthymematic and enthymematic speech.* The preponderance of unique, positive statements in the account of David and Solomon, in contrast to the distribution of enthymematic statements, reveals an effective rhetorical strategy. Initially the speech material simply supports the portrayal of the Davidic–Solomonic paradigm without directly stating the enthymeme through the employment of positive non-enthymematic statements. These statements illustrate: David's innocence (1 Chron. 12.17), God's and 'all Israel's' support of David's kingship (1 Chron. 12.18), David's concern for the ark (1 Chron. 13.2-3), his turning to God in time of battle (1 Chron. 14.10), his orders regarding proper cultic procedure (1 Chron. 15.2, 12-13), his psalm of praise (1 Chron. 16.8-36), his confession of wrong-doing and repentance (1 Chron. 21.8, 13, 17), and so on. In contrast, only a few times, and those after the paradigmatic picture has begun to develop, is the enthymeme stated in a speech during the Davidic–Solomonic period (13 times; 3 explicitly). The first speech implying the enthymeme occurs in the mouth of Yahweh in response to David's desire to build the temple (1 Chron. 17.1-15).[1] The enthymeme is then reinforced in David's answering prayer (vv. 16-27) and later clearly presented in David's closing speeches (1 Chron. 22.7-19; 28.2-10).[2] Again in the Davidic–Solomonic period, the enthymeme is directly stated in Solomon's prayer dedicating the temple (2 Chron. 6.14-42)

---

[1] This is the first occasion in the narrative proper. The maxim is actually implicitly presented in a prayer and narrative context in the opening genealogies (1 Chron. 4.9-10).

[2] Although separated, these speeches, which concern David's preparations for the temple, are part of an *inclusio* bracketing list material about cultic personnel.

and in Yahweh's reply (2 Chron. 7.12-22). However, once the Chronicler moves to the period of the succeeding Davidic kings, his argument occurs more frequently (23 times; 14 explicitly).

The employment and distribution of positive non-enthymematic statements first establishes the Chronicler's paradigm and argument inductively before it is explicitly presented and stressed. In other words, the Chronicler sets forth the supporting evidence before confronting the audience with a direct statement of the argument, the enthymeme. Rhetorically this is significant. By this means of structuring and presenting the argument, there is less dependence on the authority of the speaker (either the Chronicler or the narrative character) when the enthymeme is later openly stated. It comes more as a conclusion than as a proposition. Had the enthymeme been advanced without the accompanying and preceding supportive data, the credibility of the Chronicler would have been open to greater question. Once the Chronicler first set up the Davidic–Solomonic paradigm and then introduced his enthymeme, he had greater freedom to state it openly in his account of the Davidic kings. In short, the Davidic–Solomonic period established the enthymeme; the period of the succeeding Davidic kings illustrated it.

(4) *Function of Speeches in Relationship to the Speaker*
The person to whom a speech is attributed and his ethos also bear consideration. With a few exceptions, the speeches occur in the mouths of authoritative characters: kings (55 times), prophets (17), God (8; 2 of these are quotations).

(a) *Divine speeches.*[1] Two observations need to be made regarding the divine speeches. The first time the enthymeme is stated in a speech in Chronicles it is spoken by Yahweh in response to David's desire to build the temple (1 Chron. 17.4-14), a synoptic section containing material parallel to 2 Samuel 7. To be sure, it is not as fully and succinctly expressed as in later speeches, but it is formulated sufficiently to be drawn upon and developed further: as David desires to build a house for Yahweh, so will Yahweh establish David's house on

---

[1] See List 4 in the Appendix.

the throne forever (see particularly v. 12).[1] Without appeal to the authority of his own person, the Chronicler as rhetor built his case on an accepted cornerstone. The appeal is to the credibility of Yahweh and to a well-known tradition, not to the credibility of the narrator.

It is also noteworthy that Chronicles contains no unique speech occasions of Yahweh. All divine speeches occur in synoptic sections, although some of them do manifest various differences from their parallels.[2] Although it is true there are no unique occasions where Yahweh speaks directly, there are unique occasions where Yahweh speaks indirectly through the mouths of prophets.[3] The source for these 'new' words of Yahweh (new in our knowledge of the tradition) rests not with the Chronicler but with the prophets who are cited. One might conclude that here is revealed a constraint on the Hebrew historiographer of the Chronicler's generation. The Chronicler felt some freedom to present 'new' speeches of human characters, but not of Yahweh.

(b) *Royal prayers*.[4] Of the fifty-five occasions of royal speech occasions, nine are prayers, twenty-one are speeches proper, and twenty-five are statements. By definition, royal prayers illustrate the enthymeme, simply because the one praying is seeking God. Four of these prayers are unique to Chronicles. Both David and Solomon state the enthymeme in their conversations with Yahweh (1 Chron. 17.16-27; 2 Chron. 6.14-

---

[1] In the following prayer of David's (17.16-27), which also consists primarily of synoptic material, this theme is highlighted. The 'addition' in verse 24 of the word 'confirmed/supported' (אמן) illuminates the reciprocal nature of the enthymeme more clearly: as Yahweh's name is confirmed, so, too, the house of David is established (כון).

[2] The most significant 'addition' is found in Yahweh's response to Solomon's prayer at the dedication of the temple (2 Chron. 7.12-22), where the principle of turning to and seeking God in times of calamity is emphasized (vv. 12b-15). This has been accomplished by using synoptic material from Solomon's prayer in ch. 6, to which has been added the key terms 'seek' (בקש) and 'humble' (כנע). Once again, the Chronicler has supported his case with key traditional material.

[3] These occasions will be examined in Section 4e, 'Prophetic speeches'.

[4] See List 5 in the Appendix.

42). The content of this material is largely in verbatim accord with the parallel tradition in Samuel–Kings, although in David's prayer there is the 'addition' in v. 24 of the word 'confirmed/supported' (אמן) which highlights the enthymeme. As stated above, the first time it is presented by a human character, the character is David, the setting is prayer/conversation with Yahweh, and the material is a parallel tradition. As a result, the Chronicler established his argument with material and in a form that did not permit the authority of his own personage to be challenged.

(c) *Royal speeches*.[1] There are twenty-one royal speeches, of which seventeen are unique. Of the four in synoptic passages two contain much unique material (2 Chron. 2.3-10, 11-16), while the other two have some significant statements that are unique.[2] In contrast to some of the royal statements, all of the royal speeches proper present the king in a positive light. (Although two of the speeches are by non-Israelite royalty, Huram [2 Chron. 2.11-16] and the queen of Sheba [2 Chron. 9.5-8], even their speeches contain praise for the Israelite king, Solomon.) All of the speeches by the Davidic kings except one, 1 Chron. 12.17, either express a concern regarding the worship of Yahweh or exhort others to fear or trust him. Ten of the royal speeches restate the enthymeme in either its positive or negative form.

Four of the unique enthymematic speeches occur in the mouth of David in highly structured and rhetorically effective passages (1 Chron. 22.7-16, 18-19; 28.2-8, 9-10). They occur after David had been portrayed as one who sought Yahweh and was blessed by him; and they occur after the enthymeme had been 'privately' communicated by Yahweh to David and restated by David to Yahweh in prayer. Here, in the final speeches of David, the enthymeme is delivered to the narrative audience of Solomon and the leaders of Israel in the form

---

[1] See List 6 in the Appendix.
[2] In 2 Chron. 6.1-11, there is a statement about Yahweh not having selected a leader before David (which leaves Saul out of the picture), and about Yahweh's selection of Jerusalem for the cultic focal point (vv. 5b-6a). In the Queen of Sheba's speech (2 Chron. 9.5-8), there is an 'added' reference to Solomon's wisdom (v. 6) and the statement that Solomon is king for Yahweh, who established (עמד) Israel (v. 8).

of royal commands about Solomonic succession and the building of the temple. Containing similar material, they form an *inclusio* bracketing lis primarily of cultic personnel. This sequence of speeches should have made an impact on the audience, one in which the Chronicler's principle was clearly and emphatically proclaimed in the words of David and invested with his authority. Two conclusions can be based on this evidence. First, it is quite clear that royal speeches played a major role in stating and supporting the Chronicler's argument. And, secondly, if these speeches were created by the Chronicler, he believed that greater 'literary license' was acceptable in handling royal speeches than divine speeches.

(d) *Royal statements*.[1] There remain twenty-five royal statements. These single statements have a minor function in Chronicles.[2] For the most part, discussion of them and their functions fall under the same categories as non-enthymematic statements handled above. Of the eighteen that are unique, thirteen (eight by David) present the king in a positive light as one concerned about worshiping Yahweh properly, repenting of evil, or seeking the will of Yahweh through a prophet. Of the seven synoptic statements, three demonstrate a positive character. Again, the bulk of them function to illustrate the character of the kings according to the Chronicler's paradigm.

Besides illustrating whether a king deserved to be blessed or forsaken by Yahweh, many of these single statements serve another function in the narrative. Thirteen of these statements have no specified audience.[3] Appearing in the narrative to be directed by the speaker to himself, these comments actually explain to the Chronicler's audience why something happened. They are directed more to the intended audience than to anyone in the narrative. As such, they keep the audience from becoming side-tracked by an unexplained feature and help to move the narrative along. This device is common

---

[1] See List 7 in the Appendix.

[2] The observation that statements have a minor function is due largely to our definition that distinguished statements from speeches proper on the basis of their brevity and lesser role.

[3] 1 Chron. 11.6, 17; 13.12; 14.11; 15.2; 19.2; 22.1, 5; 23.25-26; 28.19; 2 Chron. 8.11; 12.6; 28.23.

to Samuel–Kings as well and is found in some of the synoptic texts. However, the types of matters explained differ between the synoptic texts and the unique texts. For example, the synoptic texts answer the following unresolved issues: After the first disaster with the transportation of the ark, why did David not continue to bring it to Jerusalem (1 Chron. 13.12)? How did Baal-perazim get its name (1 Chron. 14.11)? Why did David send men to an Ammonite king (1 Chron. 19.2)? These questions are rather neutral in tone; they do not have a thematic significance. In contrast, several of the statements in the Chronicler's unique material answer questions involving the cult and provide motives for actions of the kings: Why did the first attempt to transport the ark meet with failure (1 Chron. 15.2 in conjunction with 15.12-13, which has the Levites as the specified audience, but also speaks to the Chronicler's intended audience)? Why was it necessary for David to make preparations for the temple, when he was not allowed to be the one to build it (1 Chron. 22.5)? Why was it necessary to create new divisions among the cultic personnel (1 Chron. 23.25-26)? How and why did David provide plans for the temple (1 Chron. 28.19)? What was Solomon's motive for building Pharaoh's daughter a separate house (2 Chron. 8.11; note that he is exonerated by the 'answer')? Why did Ahaz build an altar and sacrifice to the gods of Damascus (2 Chron. 28.23)?

There are also more specialized narrative functions for two of these statements. Immediately following the events which led to the acquisition of land for the temple (1 Chron. 21), David says (to no one in particular), 'This is the house of Yahweh God, and this is the altar of burnt offering for Israel' (22.1). This statement helps the audience to overcome an awkward transition in the narrative from a linear-moving historical survey, in which the paradigm and enthymeme have been presented subtly, to a static section of speeches and lists setting forth cultic concerns and directly communicating the enthymeme. It introduces the temple as the topic of focus and thus provides a link from ch. 21, about how the land for the temple was acquired, to the following material about David's preparations for the temple.

Another special (and informative) case is found in 2 Chron. 12.7-8, an instance of a prophetic statement. This statement resolves an apparent contradiction between the Chronicler's principle of blessing/punishment and what actually happened. After Rehoboam had forsaken Yahweh and, consistent to the paradigm, had been forsaken to Shishak of Egypt (v. 5), he and the princes of Israel humbled themselves (v. 6). The historical reality, that was presumably known to the audience, was that Israel was not delivered completely out of the hands of Shishak, but suffered from subjugation. The audience might raise the question: How is this outcome consistent with the principle that Yahweh will restore his favor to the one who turns and humbles himself (cf. 2 Chron. 7.14)? The answer is actually provided before the question can be raised in vv. 7-8:

> ... the word of Yahweh came to Shemaiah saying, 'They have humbled themselves so I will not destroy them, but I will grant them some deliverance, and my wrath shall not be poured out on Jerusalem by means of Shishak. But they will become his slaves so that they may distinguish my service from the service of the kingdoms of the lands.'

It is unclear here whether Yahweh is speaking to Shemaiah or Shemaiah to an unspecified audience.[1] Whichever is the case, the intended audience, the rhetor's audience, now has the explanation: deliverance occurred, since the Israelites were not destroyed, but it was only partial so that they could learn a lesson. The significance of this statement lies not just in the fact that it is an example of the Chronicler protecting his maxim from being invalidated. It also reveals that the Chronicler expected his audience to have some historical knowledge and that, therefore, he could not alter the historical record to suit his own ends. Again, the theological interpretation of the outcome was supported by prophetic authority and not the narrator's authority.

(e) *Prophetic speeches.*[2] As has been frequently noted by others, prophets and prophetic speeches play an important role in Chronicles. The prophetic word was active during the Davidic–Solomonic period: confirming David's leadership (1 Chron. 11.3; 12.18), confirming David's desire to build the

---

[1] The direct quotation is introduced by, '(then) the word of Yahweh was/became to Shemaiah' (היה דבר יהוה אל שמעיה).

[2] See List 8 in the Appendix.

temple (1 Chron. 17.1-15), and pronouncing Yahweh's judgment against David for the census (1 Chron. 21.9-13).
Prophetic word foretold the division of the kingdom (2 Chron.
10.15). During the reigns of the subsequent Davidic kings,
prophets warned (11.3), rebuked (12.5), exhorted (15.2-7),
foretold judgment (16.7-9), gave instructions regarding battle
(20.15-17; 25.7-9), and foretold the outcome of battle (18.12-
27). Prophets sent by Yahweh were to be trusted and heeded
(2 Chron. 20.20), for failure to listen resulted in judgment
(2 Chron. 25.15-16). Generally, however, they met with abuse
and suffering (2 Chron. 16.10; 24.21-22; 25.16; 36.15-16).
Prophetic activity is also recorded even when their words are
not quoted (1 Chron. 11.3; 2 Chron. 10.15; 26.5; 32.20; 33.18;
36.15-16, and probably alluded to in 33.10). J. Newsome summarized the role of prophets in Chronicles thus:

> In executing his portrait of the nature and import of prophetic
> activity, the Chronicler retraced many of the lines drawn by the
> deuteronomic historians before him and he relied upon certain
> colors lying upon the common palette of the general Hebrew
> religious experience. The prophet is, above all, the spokesman
> for God. He receives the divine word and transmits it to king
> and/or people in such a way that the prophetic word is tanta-
> mount to the word of God himself. The special relationship
> between God and Israel is the single factor which permeates all
> prophecy for the Chronicler... Israel might express her devo-
> tion to Yahweh in the cult of the Jerusalem Temple, but God's
> intentions for his people were expressed primarily in the
> prophetic word. This, of course, is the reason that, for the
> Chronicler, prophecy is such a deadly serious matter. To attune
> a sensitive ear to the prophet meant life, to be deaf to him meant
> death.[1]

Further exploration of the relationship of prophetic speeches
to the presentation of the Chronicler's argument is suggestive.
There are eighteen prophetic speeches, fourteen of which are
unique. In thirteen of these speeches the key enthymeme is
either explicitly stated or implied. All thirteen cases occur after
the Davidic–Solomonic period, in which the enthymeme was
established primarily by inductive means. Osborne observed
that in the narratives about the post-Solomonic kings there

---

[1] Newsome, 'The Chronicler's View of Prophecy', pp. 222-23.

are seven basic motifs related to the Chronicler's theology of salvation around which these narratives are constructed. The fifth and sixth motifs he identified are prophetic speeches and the responses to them.[1] The Davidic kings are rebuked or have a judgment pronounced against them by a prophet when they fail to seek Yahweh properly. These prophetic speeches function as a deductive teaching tool, pointing out not just to the royal audience of the prophet, but also to the Chronicler's audience, the divine, cause–effect principle operating in the universe. Further, these prophetic speeches, in contrast to those in Samuel–Kings, emphasize the conditional nature of blessing/judgment.[2] According to the theology of the Chronicler, although forsaking Yahweh resulted in being forsaken, the possibility always seemed to remain to humble oneself, return to Yahweh, and once more receive his favor.

(5) *Summary*

The Chronicler employed speeches, set in the past and in the mouths of authoritative characters, to address forcefully his present audience while remaining personally remote. This is to say that the Chronicler employed the ethos of the characters who spoke to give an authoritative tone to the themes he wished to inculcate in his audience. These characters in the past speak authoritatively to the Chronicler's audience in their present setting. Many of the cases of direct speech either communicated the enthymeme explicitly or implicitly, or they supported the paradigm which illustrated it. The communication of the enthymeme developed from a relatively safe and subtle presentation to a direct and repeated proclamation: Yahweh was the first to give it expression, and that in synoptic material; David put it in the form of command; and the prophets repeatedly reminded one of it. Even brief single speech statements promoted the themes, hurdled problems,

---

[1] Osborne, 'The Genealogies of 1 Chronicles 1–9', pp. 39-51.

[2] These speeches are: 2 Chron. 12.5-8; 15.1-7; 16.7-10; 19.2-3; 21.12-15 (in part). According to Westermann's form-critical analysis, prophetic judgments of an earlier period were unconditional in nature, whereas in Chronicles some of the prophetic speeches reveal a formal difference in which the announcement of judgment was no longer unconditional (Westermann, pp. 163-64).

and moved the narrative. Through this rhetorical style, the narrator remains hidden and yet makes an ethical appeal to his audience, persuading them that the message is authoritative and that he is reliable.

3. *Unique material II: Evaluatory Narrative Comments*[1]

Narrative comments break into the flow of a story and supply an explanation for something or give the audience necessary data to better comprehend the events or characters. When such comments provide not just information but rather the narrator's evaluation or explanation of something, then the narrator's presence, which might have been relatively unnoticed up to that point, is felt by the audience. How greatly this intrusion would have been noticed is difficult to evaluate. Some of the narrative comments in Chronicles are verbally identical to the related passage in Samuel–Kings; others are unique. To gain some perspective on what such narrative comments might reveal about the character of the Chronicler, our focus will be on the most intrusive comments, that is, those which are unique and which provide an evaluation or explanation stating the seeking enthymeme.

As mentioned, within the genealogical prologue are a few narrative comments which foretell the Chronicler's operative principle. Once the narrative proper begins, a form of this argument is clearly articulated in an evaluative comment unique to the Chronicler. It occurs at the closing of the report of Saul's death:

> And Saul died for his sin which he sinned against Yahweh on account of the word of Yahweh which he did not keep, and even by asking the medium to seek. But he did not seek Yahweh, so he killed him and he turned over the kingdom to David the son of Jesse (1 Chron. 10.13-14).

This is a rather bold explanatory comment. The rhetor's character as a reliable interpreter is placed on the line. However, as has been observed in Chapter 2, the Chronicler was on fairly safe ground. His evaluative comment does not contradict the tradition given in Samuel–Kings. In fact it alludes to

[1] See List 1 in the Appendix.

Saul's presumptuous offering in 1 Sam. 13.9 and to the medium he consulted in 1 Sam. 28.8.

Following the same pattern that was found with enthymematic speech material, the rest of the explanatory comments which occur in the account of David and Solomon are not so bold. They do not restate the enthymeme so clearly. Rather, as the Chronicler turns to an inductive form of argumentation to create the Davidic–Solomonic paradigm, explanatory comments are used to support the construction of the paradigm. For example: David became king according to the word of Yahweh (1 Chron. 11.3); all Israel came to support him (1 Chron. 11.10; 12.22, 23, 38-40); the Levites had success because God helped them (1 Chron. 15.26); David died at an old age with riches and honor (1 Chron. 29.28-30); Solomon succeeded him and was exalted, because God was with him (2 Chron. 1.1), achieving peace, wealth and honor.

After the paradigm is complete, the succeeding Davidic monarchs are either explicitly or implicitly compared to this model. The stories become more like evaluatory reports with frequent intrusive comments. These narrative comments now support the main enthymeme stated at the death of Saul. They either restate it or they clarify how a following or preceding event illustrates the principle of seeking that is operating within the history of Israel (20 out of 27 cases). These comments are the nudgings of the narrator to persuade the audience to accept his argument as valid over the whole course of Israelite history. Their effectiveness rests on the ethical appeal of the Chronicler.

The Chronicler's presentation of his argument follows this pattern: the enthymeme is first foreshadowed in comments in the genealogical prologue; then at the beginning of the narrative proper, it is presented deductively in a rather safe explanatory comment; it is further argued inductively through the example of David and Solomon; and finally, once the paradigm is established, the enthymeme is repeatedly argued deductively in the form of evaluatory comments (and prophetic speeches). Strategically, the Chronicler's dependence on an ethical appeal, an appeal to the reliability of this evaluation, comes after his case has been well established inductively and in the midst of further illustrations.

C. *Conclusion*

In summary of these observations regarding the ethical mode of persuasion, it has been noted:

1. Although only tentative, some conclusions about the Chronicler's use of traditional material can be suggested. The Chronicler achieved a new portrayal of the past mainly by rearranging and omitting parallel material, rather than by contradicting important traditions. These modifications probably would not have appeared obtrusive or contradictory to his audience. When the Chronicler brought in cultic practices or recorded events in terms of cultic laws, his cultic priority, his interpretive techniques, and his hermeneutic would have been shared by and respected by his post-exilic audience. These characteristics probably would have raised the audience's esteem for the narrator rather than lowered it.

2. The bulk of Chronicles that is 'new' material, to our perspective, has the nature of being external proofs. This is to say that the Chronicler did not just rely on the authority of his voice as historical narrator; he brought in outside, authoritative evidence. He incorporated 'objective', statistical data in the form of lists and genealogies. He 'recorded' speeches made by authoritative characters: Davidic kings, prophets of God, and Yahweh himself. More than just imported, this material was strategically shaped and placed to support the Chronicler's argument. As a result, in particular regard to the speeches, the Chronicler was often able to remain 'behind the scenes', speak through the mouth of his characters, and employ their ethos, their authority.

3. The Chronicler himself spoke in an authoritative style, in the omniscient and unobtrusive voice of a historical narrator. He never used first-person speech or directly called attention to himself. His story purports to be the history of Judah 'as it actually happened'. His presence as narrator comes closest to the surface in his unique, explanatory comments. Yet, even these are employed cautiously and judiciously so that not much rests on the authority of his

voice until after the main argument is presented and supported by other means.

These devices all have a cumulative effect. In terms of his own ethos, the Chronicler seems to display good sense, good character, and good will. And, stylistically, he spoke in an authoritative manner. But, what is most important to notice is that to create a weight of reliability for his narrative of Israel's history, the Chronicler confronted the audience with a mosaic of authoritative 'witnesses': his voice, known tradition, the voices of kings and prophets, and objective data. In conclusion, the Chronicler, presented with the problem of retelling a story known to his audience, effectively used the ethical mode of persuasion as a part of his rhetorical strategy.

Chapter 5

PATHOS: THE EMOTIONAL MODE OF PERSUASION

A. *Introduction*

Pathos is the third of the three *pisteis*. It is the mode of artistic persuasion which occurs when the audience is moved through the speech to emotion. The emotions of the hearers must not be overlooked, for, as Aristotle said, 'Our judgments when we are pleased and friendly are not the same as when we are pained and hostile'.[1] Contrary to what one might first suppose, Aristotle's treatment of the emotional mode of persuasion involves the material of the speech and not the orator's delivery. Furthermore, Aristotle differed with some of his contemporaries over the role of pathos in rhetoric. They regarded pathos as an element of a speech designed to play on the emotions of an audience and relegated it to the introduction. For Aristotle the pathos appeal was viewed as an artistic appeal belonging with the development of the rational argument.[2] In fact, the emotional appeal is integral to the topoi of the logos appeal.[3] This is to say, one could use certain enthymematic forms of argumentation to evoke the desired emotional response, such as: 'Since A is Z, you ought to feel Y'. Or, one could use emotions as part of the content of an argument: 'He,

---

[1] Aristotle, I. 2. 1356a13-16.
[2] Arnhart, p. 22; Kennedy, *Persuasion*, pp. 93-95. Arnhart (p. 114) has clarified the rational side of emotions: 'The success of the rhetorician in handling the passions suggests that the passions must somehow be rational. For in trying to persuade an audience to adhere to some passion and give up others, the speaker must assume that speech alone is sufficient to alter men's passion.'
[3] Thomas Conley, *'Pathe* and *Pisteis*: Aristotle, "Rhetoric", II, 2-11', *Hermes* 110/3 (1982), pp. 300-15.

not I, probably killed B, because it was he who was an *echthros* [enemy] of B, while I was a *philos* [friend]'.[1]

The pathos appeal is very similar to the ethos appeal in the manner in which it complements the rational appeal. Both are concerned with the emotive responses which influence the decisions the audience makes about the speaker and the content of the speech. Aristotle explained:

> But since rhetoric exists to affect the giving of decisions—the hearers decide between one political speaker and another, and a legal verdict *is* a decision—the orator must not only try to make the argument of his speech demonstrative and worthy of belief; he must also make his own character look right [ethos appeal] and put his hearers, who are to decide, into the right frame of mind [pathos appeal]... When people are feeling friendly and placable, they think one sort of thing; when they are feeling angry or hostile, they think either something totally different or the same thing with a different intensity... Again, if they are eager for, and have good hopes of, a thing that will be pleasant if it happens, they think that it certainly will happen and be good for them: whereas if they are indifferent or annoyed, they do not think so.[2]

To make this appeal artfully, the rhetor must understand the nature of the emotions and what arouses them. Therefore, Aristotle devoted a part of his treatise (II. 2–11) to a systematic explanation of the emotions. In his analysis of each emotion he gave attention to three features:

> The Emotions are all those feelings that so change men as to affect their judgments, and that are also attended by pain or pleasure. Such are anger, pity, fear and the like, with their opposites. We must arrange what we have to say about each of them under three heads. Take, for instance, the emotion of anger: here we must discover (1) what the state of mind of angry people is, (2) who the people are with whom they usually get angry, and (3) on what grounds they get angry with them. It is not enough to know one or even two of these points; unless we know all three, we shall be unable to arouse anger in any one. The same is true of the other emotions.[3]

---

[1] *Ibid.*, p. 309.
[2] Aristotle, II. 1. 1377b21-1378a5; the comments in brackets are mine.
[3] Aristotle, II. 1. 1378a20-28.

Employing his three-part analysis, Aristotle then explored: anger and calmness, friendship and enmity, fear, shame and shamelessness, kindness and unkindness, pity and indignation, envy, and emulation.

The goal of this chapter is to observe the ways in which the Chronicler has told his story so as to affect the emotions of the audience in a manner sympathetic to his argument. Since many of these means are achieved through features of Chronicles which have been discussed in the previous chapters, the treatment of pathos can be set forth in a brief form.

B. *Analysis*

1. *Themes and Motifs*

One of the obvious means by which the Chronicler sought to evoke an emotional response was through the development and employment of words and phrases with emotional connotations. The Chronicler employed these emotive words and phrases to induce the desired feelings toward the objects of his focus, the kings, the cult, and the principle of blessing/punishment. Leslie Allen has drawn attention to the fact that the books of Chronicles in several places can be divided into short units in which a certain word or phrase occurs in the role of an *inclusio*, recurring motif, or contrasted motif.[1] For example, in 1 Chronicles 11–12, which relates the groups of 'mighty men' who gave their support to David, the verb עזר ('help') and compounds formed with it occur fifteen times.[2] As a result, not just the divine blessing, but also the human help for the king is accentuated.[3] Such repeated phrases create evaluative associations with the kings and their activities. The phrase 'all Israel' occurs often in the greater unit on David and Solomon, where its impact is to elevate their stature as ones who elicited the united support of 'all Israel'.[4] Both 'good' and 'bad' kings

---

[1] Allen, 'Kerygmatic Units'.

[2] 11.12, 28; 12.1, 3, 7(× 2), 10, 18, 19(× 2), 20, 22, 23, 34, 39 (*ibid.*, pp. 7-8).

[3] *Ibid.*, pp. 8-9. The use of עזר in this section was also observed by Rudolph (*Chronikbücher*, p. 105), Williamson ('Setting and Purpose', pp. 166-67), and Willi (p. 224).

[4] 1 Chron. 11.1, 4, 10; 12.38; 13.5, 6, 8; 14.8; 15.3, 28; 18.14; 19.17; 28.4; 29.23, 25, 26; 2 Chron. 1.2; 5.3; 7.3, 8; 9.30.

have such stereotypical language employed in the account of their reigns. As a result, a patriotic audience ought to respond with feelings of pride and favor for their heroic forefathers and with embarrassment toward the baser characters in their national history.

In association with the cult, two main motifs stand out. The first motif regards the authoritative basis of the cultic institutions. These institutions were not just established by the heroic figures of David and Solomon, a feature which stands in contrast to the 'silence' about the origin of such institutions in Samuel–Kings. Their ultimate justification is based on divine disclosure originally made to Moses and recorded in the book of law (1 Chron. 6.49, 15.15; 22.13; 2 Chron. 8.13; 23.18; 24.9; 30.16; 34.14-21) as well as directly to David (1 Chron. 28.11-19). As a result, the audience's respect for and feelings toward Mosaic revelation, as well as toward the Chronicler's larger-than-life David and Solomon, are shifted toward the cultic institutions of their day. The second motif regards inner feelings toward cultic activities. In the Chronicler's portrayal of character, as with most Hebrew narrative characterization, the inner feelings of characters are usually not mentioned by the narrator but implied by their actions or revealed in their speech.[1] However, there is one type of activity in Chronicles which is frequently associated with an expression of feeling: cultic activities are carried out with singing and joy.[2] Here the Chronicler depicted the proper emotional response toward participation in the cult of Yahweh.

Certainly the Chronicler also designed his presentation of the law of retribution to incite specific feelings. 'To seek Yahweh', which probably carried some emotional overtones already at its first occurrence, developed into an emotionally charged concept by the end of the narrative. 'To seek Yahweh'

---

[1] A. Berlin, *Poetics and Interpretation of Biblical Narrative* (Sheffield: Almond, 1983), pp. 34-41; R. Alter, *The Art of Biblical Narrative* (New York: Basic Books, 1981), chapter 6, 'Characterization and the Art of Reticence'.

[2] 1 Chron. 13.6-8; 15.16-29; 29.9, 22; 2 Chron. 5.12-13; 15.14-15; 20.21-22, 27-28; 23.18; 29.25-30; 30.21, 25-26. Braun ('Significance', p. 185) observed that שׂמח (rejoice) occurs fifteen times in Chronicles without parallel in Samuel–Kings.

evokes thoughts of blessing, that is, the 'good things' of life which would be desired by the Chronicler's intended audience: peace or at least victory in war, prosperity, and security. On the other hand, 'to abandon/forsake/disobey Yahweh' do not simply denote neutral actions. Since such actions result in defeat and humiliation, they call up thoughts of disaster and feelings of despair.

2. *Character Portrayal and Typology*

The Chronicler's style of characterization also conveys a pathos appeal. He employed typology both for an authoritative and emotive effect.[1] Not only has it long been noted that 'good' Davidic kings follow the pattern set by David and Solomon, but it also has been observed that Solomon's succession to David was patterned after Joshua's succession to Moses,[2] that Solomon's and Hiram's role in building the temple have parallels to Bezalel and Oholiab,[3] and that even the account of building the temple follows a stereotypical pattern found in the ancient Near East.[4] Through the use of this literary device the audience's evaluation of, and feelings for, the prototypical character or event are carried over to the secondary character or event. Joshua's succession of Moses, which was a God-ordained, foundational event, probably prompted feelings of nationalistic pride and loyal support. When Solomon's succession is recorded with similar phrases, one can expect that an informed audience would make the association and carry over some of the same feelings to the new portrayal.

Reinforcing this typological characterization is the fact that the characters, for the most part, are portrayed in a polar negative/positive fashion. Saul is painted negatively. He is the prototype of the wicked monarch as well as the foil for David.

---

[1] See Alter, chapter 3, 'Biblical Type-Scenes and the Uses of Convention'.

[2] Braun, 'Significance', pp. 30-34, and 'Solomon, the Chosen Temple Builder: The Significance of 1 Chronicles 22, 28, and 29 for the Theology of Chronicles', *JBL* 95 (1976), pp. 586-88; Dillard, 'The Chronicler's Solomon', pp. 293-95.

[3] Dillard, 'The Chronicler's Solomon', pp. 296-99.

[4] A.S. Kapelrud, 'Temple Building, a Task for Gods and Kings', *Or* 32 (1963), pp. 56-62.

With the exception of David's act of taking the census, the Chronicler depicted David and Solomon as faultless rulers who had the correct relationship with Yahweh. Also, the evaluative explanatory comments found in the accounts of the kings generally concluded that the king either sought Yahweh or did evil. It is true that a reversal could and did take place in the lives of some of the Davidic monarchs; nevertheless, their actions at any one time were either right or wrong. There is no middle ground. As a result the 'proper' negative or positive feelings toward a character are evoked and reinforced without room for ambiguity.

3. *Emplotment: The Kind of Story Told*

Because of the narrow temporal parameters in which the Chronicler's paradigm is repeated, he produced a certain kind of story with an emotional effect. Each account of a Davidic king was presented as a separate unit, as a separate 'frame' or 'slice' of history. The divine, causal law of blessing/punishment was operative in and virtually limited to each individual unit. The Chronicler did not present a fatalistic, downward course of history in which several generations received the consequences of their forefather's unrighteous actions. Such a story would leave an audience in any negative circumstances with little optimism for a better life. The divine law which was evoked by the actions of a king and his people could be reversed by the opposite actions. Each generation could expect a reversal of blessing or judgment within their own generation. As a result, the kind of story the Chronicler told was, in the classical sense, a 'romantic' one which presented a view of history offering the prospect of a happy ending. One could, in a sense, always return to the conditions of the 'Golden Age' of David and Solomon by modeling these heroes. In times of blessing, there was a need for steadfastness; in times of disaster, a foundation for hope.

4. *The Argument: Maxims and Historical Examples*

The Chronicler's manner of demonstrating his argument also served as a means through which an emotional appeal is made. The deductive form in which the Chronicler expressed his argument tends to have more emotive impact than the full enthymematic form. Aristotle noted that to express character or to create passion it was better to argue with maxims rather than with the full enthymeme.[1] Aristotle's general rule was to abbreviate enthymemes as much as possible. When using widely accepted principles, there is no need to become tedious and state the complete case.[2] And, in fact, Aristotle recognized that it is generally more persuasive to develop something which one's audience already accepted as a general truth:

> One great advantage of maxims to a speaker is due to the want of intelligence in his hearers, who love to hear him succeed in expressing as a universal truth the opinions which they hold themselves about particular cases... The maxim... is a general statement, and people love to hear stated in general terms what they already believe in some particular connexion: e.g. if a man happens to have bad neighbours or bad children, he will agree with any one who tells him, 'Nothing is more annoying than having neighbours', or, 'Nothing is more foolish than to be the parents of children'. The orator has therefore to guess the subjects on which his hearers really hold views already, and what those views are, and then must express, as general truths, these same views on these same subjects.[3]

Therefore, rather than stating the full enthymeme, it is not only sufficient, but also more emotionally evocative for the Chronicler to state, 'He [Saul] did not seek Yahweh, and (therefore) he caused him to die' (1 Chron. 10.14). Here, the maxim is understood to be the negative counterpart of: 'Yahweh blesses those who seek him'. There is no need to state the full enthymeme:

> Yahweh punishes those who fail to seek him.
> Saul did not seek Yahweh.
> Therefore, Saul was punished by Yahweh.

The abbreviated form builds on what the audience has already accepted and it has a more direct emotional impact.

The Chronicler's inductive approach, through repeated examples from the past, also generates an emotional impact.

---

[1] Aristotle, III. 17. 1418a12-21.
[2] Aristotle, I. 2. 1357a17-21 and II. 22. 1395b20-31. For a fuller discussion, see Ryan (pp. 41-46)
[3] Aristotle, II. 21. 1395b1-13.

Through the creation of his paradigm and through the for-
mulaic structure of the lives of the Davidic kings, the Chronicler demonstrated a pattern found in the history of Israel.
Numerous examples of patterning are found in the history-
telling of ancient Hebrew and Jewish literature from the
Hebrew Bible to the writings of the Qumran community to the
Gospels of the New Testament.[1] To those of this mindset, it
appears that patterns in history carried a certain weight. If
something happened once in a particular way, it was likely to
happen again. That the Chronicler could demonstrate a pattern in Israelite history, gave a certain authority and believ-
ability (ethos) to his historical account. If this pattern was
accepted by the audience as operative in history, feelings of
anticipation or apprehension (pathos) would be present as
they examined their own period for manifestations of the pattern. When divine activity was the subject of such patterns,
these patterns then should have elicited a security in the con-
tinuity and predictability of divine behavior toward Israel.

5. *Direct Address through Speeches*
As has been remarked in the discussion on ethos, speeches
pack a powerful rhetorical influence. Although addressed to
characters within the narrative world, when speeches are
'quoted' directly, they have the impact of including the story-
teller's external audience as addressees along with the audience internal to the story. When David or a prophet exhorts
their audience, the Chronicler's audience, too, receives the
exhortation. By this means, the Chronicler's audience has
been encouraged throughout the telling of the story by
authoritative speakers to carry out the proper course of action
as well as being upbraided for improper actions.

---

[1] For the use and effect of patterning in the Old Testament, see Alter
(chapters 3 and 5), and for the use of stereotypical presentations in
rabbinic exegesis, see Patte (pp. 67-74), who prefers to call the device
'telescoping'.

C. *Summary*

The Chronicler did not strive to give a complex presentation and evaluation of characters and events which could produce an ambiguous emotional response. The picture is clear; the desired responses are unambiguous. David and Solomon, whose actions the Chronicler would like his audience to emulate, are painted in heroic colors. They are ancestors of whom one should be proud. Wicked forefathers are a source of shame. The proper cultic attitudes and actions of the 'good' kings resulted in blessing; improper ones resulted in cursing. Such behavior set into motion a clearly defined law operative in history, the recognition of which should evoke either anxiety or confidence. One course produced the good things of life which one desired; the other course produced the things one feared. Experiencing judgment, there is hope for reversal; enjoying the fruit of blessing, there is need for steadfastness. Kings exhort; prophets rebuke. Pride versus shame, emulation versus disdain, desire for the good things of life versus apprehension over the bad, confidence versus anxiety, hope versus despair, and encouragement versus reproof—all such emotions line up with the appropriate character, action, and ideology. The audience is persuaded emotionally to accept and act on the Chronicler's argument.

Chapter 6

CONCLUSIONS

A. *Summary*

Applied to a biblical, historical narrative, the tools of a rhetorical analysis provide a new approach to understanding the artistry, function, and meaning of a text. The rhetorical features of a work are not extraneous, cosmetic elements added to enhance its appearance. They form the body of a work. It is the rhetorical nature of a work which determines its ability to communicate. This is as true for historical narratives as for other forms of communication. As Hayden White has stated, 'The principal source of a historical work's strength as an *interpretation* of the *events* which it treats as *the data to be explained* is rhetorical in nature'.[1] The rhetoric of a historical work is its principal source of appeal to the audience to accept the work.[2] Beyond simply classifying rhetorical features, one can also gain insight into the story-teller's character, world-view, theological perspective, purpose, and perceived audience.

In the books of Chronicles, we have maintained that a major purpose of the narrator was to inculcate a particular message upon which he wanted the audience to act, that is: seeking Yahweh wholeheartedly through the proper cultic means would result in blessing for Israel, whereas failure to seek Yahweh would result in disaster. Through his selection of material and particularly through the structure of his narrative, the Chronicler created a paradigm exemplifying the principle of blessing. This paradigm, achieved as well by a reduction of the elements/events in the historical field, allowed for, or rather invited, the audience to classify characters,

---

[1] White, 'Rhetoric and History', p. 3.
[2] *Ibid.*

actions, events, and periods of history in polar terms of negative or positive. Moreover, the audience is implicitly invited to take a further step and apply the analysis to their own generation. But they are not to stop at the point of self-evaluation; they are to act. The Chronicler's story-line demonstrates that the causal laws operating within reality are put into effect by human agency and are reversible from generation to generation. Conforming to the paradigm, modeling the positive characters of Israel's 'Heroic Age', David and Solomon, the audience can strive to establish and maintain the proper cultic worship and receive blessing, or they can neglect it and receive judgment.

The Chronicler stated and demonstrated his argument about seeking Yahweh several times in a variety of ways, employing the two forms of rhetorical argumentation, the enthymeme and the example. The enthymeme was built formally on a maxim of divine retribution with connective signs which would have been ideologically acceptable to his audience. Developing this principle, he redefined the actions which prompted divine blessing/punishment in terms of establishing and maintaining the cult of Yahweh. One of the primary material topics of his argument was that acting appropriately would result in the good of the nation. Although the Chronicler initially proposed his argument in the high-risk form of a narrative comment early in his story (regarding Saul's death), this first statement did not move much beyond traditionally accepted parameters. For the most part, the enthymeme is stated sparingly in the first half of the Chronicler's work, and even there it is stated by authoritative characters in their speeches and not by the Chronicler as the narrator. The accounts of the succeeding Davidic kings serve as a series of examples of the paradigm of seeking. In this second half of the work, the Chronicler proceeded with greater boldness and proclaimed the enthymeme more frequently. On a whole, the Chronicler moved from a cautious inductive presentation of his case to a more propositional or 'deductive' form of argumentation, using examples as supportive evidence.

The Chronicler was faced with the situation of how to reshape and reformulate traditional material, in order to tell the audience's story as he perceived it, without losing their confidence. Although changing, rearranging, and omitting traditional material, the Chronicler avoided obtrusive contradictions which would have confronted his audience with the need to reject one version or the other of their past. What interpretive techniques he did use (e.g. reading contemporary cultic practices into the earlier record) probably would have reflected values his audience shared and would have raised their evaluation of his character. Still, the Chronicler did not presume to speak on his own authority. The bulk of material which is 'new' to Chronicles—about one-half of the work— functions as external proofs. These lists, genealogies, and speeches, strategically shaped and placed, 'objectively' support the Chronicler's argument. Particularly through the speeches of authoritative characters, the Chronicler remained behind the scenes yet made his voice heard. When his presence rarely does surface in the form of explanatory narrative comments, his case has already been well developed by other means. In short, the Chronicler, as narrator, reveals himself as knowledgeable, reliable, and well disposed toward the interests of the audience.

The Chronicler painted his account in bold, contrasting colors with definite, unambiguous strokes intended to prompt the correct emotional response from the audience. Wicked kings and their followers receive fearful consequences. Heroic kings and their people enjoy the fruit of blessing. Pride, emulation, hope; shame, disdain, despair—each set of emotions is appropriately evoked by the stereotypical presentation of characters, actions, and events.

With skill and artistry the Chronicler retold the story of Israel in such a way as to set forth a world-view and an ideology for action within that world. Perhaps his rhetorical measures were carefully calculated and planned. Perhaps his skill was naturally and unconsciously employed. Whichever the case, the Books of Chronicles exemplify artistic persuasion.

B. *Direction for Further Reflection*

Rhetorical analyses of biblical literature can lead to fruitful applications. One such further application would be to make a comparative evaluation of the biblical historical narratives.

For example, the type of narrative material differs significantly between Chronicles and Samuel–Kings. Samuel–Kings utilizes more dialogue to achieve a fuller character presentation. More importantly, the arguments demonstrated in Samuel–Kings are built on a somewhat different world-view, with the story-line and structure presenting a tragic emplotment. There is little hope offered in the story of the monarchies for overcoming the chaotic forces of life and divine punishment. The themes of judgment for sin and accumulation of guilt stand out stronger than those of blessing and restoration. Although Solomon's dedicatory prayer for the temple offers some hope for repentance and deliverance, there are fewer illustrations of this in Samuel–Kings than in Chronicles. In Chronicles prophetic speeches of judgment are not as unconditional as in Kings;[1] the concept of turning/returning (שׁוב) is applied to turning to Yahweh, where in Kings it usually means turning away from sin;[2] and humbling oneself (כנע) regularly has a inner religious connotation in Chronicles, whereas in Samuel–Kings it has this meaning only three times, and even then it refers more to an outward action rather than to an inward attitude.[3] In Samuel–Kings, the divine, causal laws in the world operate over larger measures of time and multiple generations of people. For example, in 2 Kgs 21.10-15, once Manasseh led the people of Judah astray, a course of judgment was set in motion which could not be stopped even by a succeeding righteous king (cf. 22.26; 24.2-4). The narrator/s has/have depicted a rather mechanistic and fatalistic picture, not particularly prompting restorative actions as much as evoking shame.[4]

After a comparative rhetorical study, one might take a further step and explore what accounts for different arguments based on differing world-views which result in different historical paradigms. Victor Turner, working from the perspective of anthropology, has explored how older paradigms for social experience become mutated or replaced by newer mod-

---

[1] Schaefer, p. 30.
[2] *Ibid.*, p. 71.
[3] *Ibid.*, pp. 73-74.
[4] Fishbane (p. 380) has made a similar observation.

els for interpreting socio-cultural experiences as one passes
through liminal states, or critical points, in one's history.[1] One
suggestive approach to the issue of shifting modes of argumentation can be found in an article by Edward Bruner in
which he is concerned with the methods by which ethno-
graphers have approached the reconstruction of the history of
cultures.[2] Bruner states that behind one's conception of the
present, as well as the past and future, lies a story-line of how
segments of temporal sequence are systematically related.
Through this story-line one reconstructs the past and predicts
the future. Bruner is concerned, however, with how story-
lines change in a culture. He suggests that such story-lines
organize and give meaning to one's experience, but when
one's experience is no longer encompassed by the dominant
story, a new one can take its place and bring about, as a consequence, a re-evaluation of the past:

> Only after the new narrative becomes dominant is there a re-
> examination of the past, a re-discovery of old texts, a re-creation
> of the new heroes... The new story articulates what had been
> only dimly perceived, authenticates previous feelings, legit-
> imizes new actions, and aligns individual consciousness with a
> larger social movement.[3]

Bruner theorizes that story-lines can change in one of two
ways. With the continual retelling of a story in new contexts, it
becomes modified incrementally. But, a complete switch to a
new story can also occur when there is a radical shift in the
social context and the old story can no longer encompass the
new experiences.

It is likely that the final major redactor of Samuel–Kings, or
the Deuteronomistic History, stood in the exilic condition and
looked back on the course of events in an attempt to understand how they led up to Israel's situation. The Chronicler,
writing sometime after the return from exile, looked upon the

[1] V. Turner, *Dramas, Fields, and Metaphors: Symbolic Action in
Human Society* (Ithaca: Cornell University Press, 1974).
[2] E.M. Bruner, 'Ethnography as Narrative', *The Anthropology of
Experience* (ed. V. Turner and E.M. Bruner; Urbana: University of
Illinois, 1986), pp. 139-55.
[3] *Ibid.*, p. 143.

return as a major turn in the life of Israel, a passage through a liminal state. This experience provided him with a re-evaluation of the past, a new story-line, and a new argument about the laws at work in the reality of the present. Perhaps thinking of the words of Jeremiah (cf. 2 Chron. 36.21; Jer. 29.10-14), the Chronicler came to accept as a natural law the concept that Yahweh will redeem those who turn and humble themselves and seek him. Taken from the event of the restoration, this law provided a new paradigm, new spectacles through which the past traditions were reviewed. New 'events' were seen to exist in the older stories and traditions. Examples of the principle of seeking were discovered in the past. Elements of tradition and perhaps other records which were of little importance to the redactors of Samuel–Kings might have had great significance for the Chronicler. In short, the narrators of Samuel–Kings and Chronicles identified, selected, structured, and interpreted the elements of the historical field through different presupposed symbol systems for perceiving reality. Provided with insights gained from rhetorical and literary analyses, perhaps biblical historians can examine the biblical accounts in light of their original presupposed symbol systems and come to a fuller understanding of the mindset and theology of the writers and the communities for whom the accounts were composed.

APPENDIX

LIST 1: NARRATIVE COMMENTS WITH 'SEEKING' ENTHYMEME

Key: 1st column: location in the books of Chronicles
2nd column: U (unique material), S (synoptic), B (contains both)
3rd column: EI (enthymeme implicit) EX (enthymeme explicit)

I.2.3	S	EX	'And Er... was wicked in the sight of Yahweh, so he put him to death.' Based on a general maxim of divine retribution and an accepted sign of retribution, death.
I.5.20-22	U	EX	Reubenites, Gadites, and half-tribe of Manasseh victorious in battle, 'because they cried out to God... and he was entreated... because they trusted him.' Based on general maxim and acceptable sign of military victory.
I.5.25-26	U	EX	Reubenites, Gadites, and half-tribe of Manasseh 'acted treacherously' and 'played the harlot', so God had them carried off into exile. Based on general maxim and a traditional sign of captivity/defeat.
I.9.1	U	EI	'And Judah was carried away into exile to Babylon for their unfaithfulness.' Implicit to audience that passive verb (and tradition) recognizes that the exile was an action of Yahweh.
I.10.13-14	U	EX	'And Saul died for his sin which he sinned against Yahweh, on account of the word of Yahweh which he did not keep, and even by asking the medium to seek. But he did not seek Yahweh, so he killed him and he turned over the kingdom to David the son of Jesse.' Based on a general maxim and traditional signs, but moves toward general concept of 'seeking Yahweh'.
I.13.10	B	EX	(U reason in S section) Uzza struck down by Yahweh, 'because he put out his hand to the ark'. Principle of retribution put into effect by a cultic-related action; begins to identify the parameters of seeking and forsaking.

I.15.25-26	B	EX	(U reason in S section) Successful transportation of the ark and celebration, because God helped Levites. Blessing occurs in connection with a proper cultic action; implicitly defining concept of proper seeking.
II.13.18	U	EX	'And the sons of Israel were subdued at that time, and the sons of Judah were strong because they trusted in Yahweh, the God of their fathers.' Follows an example making explicit the relationship between cause and effect.
II.13.20	U	EI	'And Jeroboam did not again recover strength in the days of Abijah; and Yahweh struck him and he died.' Connection to an action of forsaking is implicit, since the preceding verses (4-12) portray Jeroboam as one who abandoned the cult of Yahweh.
II.14.5 (6)	U	EI	'And there was no one at war with him [Asa] during those years, because Yahweh had given him rest.' Connection to seeking implicit; follows illustrations of Asa and Judah seeking Yahweh (vv. 2-5).
II.15.15	U	EX	'And all Judah rejoiced concerning the oath [to see Yahweh (v. 12)], for with their whole heart they had sworn and with their every desire they had sought him, and he let them find him; so Yahweh gave them rest on every side.'
II.17.3-4	U	EX	'And Yahweh was with Jehoshaphat, because he followed the example of his father David's earlier days and did not seek the Baals, but sought the God of his father... So Yahweh established the kingdom in his control ... and he had great riches and honor.'
II.20.30	U	EI	'So the kingdom of Jehoshaphat was at peace, for his God gave him rest on all sides.' Immediately follows an example of seeking and military victory (vv. 1-29).
II.21.10	B	EX	(U reason in S section) 'So Edom revolted from under the hand of Judah to this day. Then Libnah revolted at the same time... because he [Jehoram] had forsaken Yahweh the God of his fathers.'
II.22.7	U	EX	'Now the destruction of Ahaziah was from God, in that he went to Joram.' Explicit, because preceding texts and the immediate context clarify that the Northern Kingdom (Joram) was idolatrous and that to make an alliance with an idolatrous nation is an act of forsaking Yahweh (cf. II.13.4-12; 16.7; 19.2; 20.37; 22.3-9).
II.24.24	U	EX	'Indeed the army of the Syrians came with a small number of men; yet Yahweh delivered a very great army [Judah's] into their hands, because they had forsaken Yahweh ... '

II.25.20	B	EX	(U reason in S account) 'But Amaziah would not listen, for it was from God, that he might deliver them into the hand (of Joash) because they had sought the gods of Edom.'
II.25.27	B	EI	(U reason in S section) 'And from the time that Amaziah turned away from following Yahweh, they conspired against him ...' Implicit to audience, because divine retribution indicated by the sign of rebellion.
II.26.5	U	EX	'And he [Uzziah] continued to seek God in the days of Zechariah ... and in the days of his seeking Yahweh, God caused him to prosper.'
II.27.6	U	EI	'Jotham became mighty because he ordered his ways before Yahweh his God.' Divine blessing is implicit to audience, because might is from God (cf. I.29.11-12).
II.28.6	B	EI	'For Pekah the son of Remaliah slew in Judah 120,000 in one day, all valiant men, because they had forsaken Yahweh the God of their fathers.' Implicit, because defeat is from Yahweh.
II.28.19	U	EX	'For Yahweh humbled Judah because of Ahaz king of Israel, for he had brought about a lack of restraint in Judah and was very unfaithful to Yahweh.'
II.28.25	U	EX	'And in every city of Judah he [Ahaz] made high places to burn incense to other gods, and provoked Yahweh, the God of his fathers, to anger.'
II.32.22	U	EI	'And Yahweh saved Hezekiah ... and gave rest [reading with LXX] to them.' After example of Hezekiah and Isaiah praying and Yahweh delivering (vv. 20-21).
II.32.26	U	EX	'Hezekiah humbled the pride of his heart, he and the inhabitants of Jerusalem; so [disjunctive waw] the wrath of Yahweh did not come on them in the days of Hezekiah.'
II.33.12-13	U	EX	'He [Manasseh] entreated Yahweh and humbled himself ... and he [Yahweh] was moved by his entreaty ... and brought him back to Jerusalem.'
II.36.15-16	U	EX	'And Yahweh ... sent to them again and again his messengers ... but they mocked the messengers of God ... until the wrath of Yahweh rose against his people ...'

LIST 2: SPEECH MATERIAL WITH 'SEEKING' ENTHYMEME

Key: 1st column: location in the books of Chronicles
2nd column: U (unique material), S (synoptic), B (contains both)
3rd column: speeches with the enthymeme labeled either EI
(enthymeme implicit) or EX (enthymeme explicit)

I.4.10	U	EI	prayer of Jabez: enthymeme implicit since one who prays seeks God and recognizes that divine intervention may result.
I.17.4-14	B	EI	God to Nathan for David: God's promise to establish Davidic dynasty in response to David's desire to build temple.
I.17.16-27	B	EI	prayer of David in response to divine promise: connection between Yahweh establishing David and David establishing Yahweh (vv. 23-24).
I.21.8	S	EI	prayer of David in response to judgment: confession of sin and request for iniquity to be removed.
I.21.17	B	EI	prayer of David in response to pestilence: accepts responsibility for sin and petitions God to spare the people.
I.22.7-16	U	EI	David's charge to Solomon: repeats God's promise, 'He shall build a house for my name... and I will establish the throne of his kingdom...'
I.22.18-19	U	EI	David's charge to the leaders: Yahweh has given rest, therefore seek Yahweh, build the temple; causal relationship implicit, defines further the nature of seeking.
I.28.2-8	U	EX	David to leaders: makes explicit the relationship of blessing to obedience (v. 7) and seeking to blessing (v. 8).
I.28.9-10	U	EX	David to Solomon: 'If you seek him, he will let you find him; but if you forsake him, he will reject you forever'. Positive and negative sides of enthymeme stated with 'seeking' connected to the cult (v. 10).
I.28.20-21	U	EI	David to Solomon: connection between Yahweh's presence and the establishment of the cult.
I.29.10-19	U	EI	praise and prayer of David: defines further the signs of blessing: power, victory, riches, honor (vv. 11-12), connection to building temple (v. 16) seeking (v. 17) and obedience (v. 18).

II.1.7-12	B	EI	dialogue between Solomon and Yahweh after Solomon had sacrificed to Yahweh: connection between seeking and the promised wisdom, wealth, and honor is implicit.
II.6.14-42	B	EI	(S with U addition of vv. 40-42) Solomon's prayer of dedication: requests Yahweh's favorable response when people turn to God in need.
II.7.12-22	B	EX	Yahweh to Solomon: U section (vv. 13-15) states enthymeme in terms of 'humbling selves', 'seeking', and 'turning'; promises continuity of dynasty on condition of walking as David walked (vv. 17-18); states negative side of forsaking as well (vv. 19-22).
II.12.5	U	EX	Shemaiah to Rehoboam (word of Yahweh): 'You have forsaken me, so even I have forsaken you into the hand of Shishak'.
II.12.7-8	U	EX	word of Yahweh through Shemaiah: because Rehoboam and the leaders humbled themselves, God will grant a partial deliverance.
II.13.4-12	U	EI	King Abijah to Jeroboam and Israel: rebukes them for rebelling against the Davidic dynasty and for forsaking Yahweh, warns them of failure.
II.14.7	U	EI	Asa to Judah: 'The land is before us, because we have sought Yahweh our God...'
II.14.11	U	EI	prayer of Asa: petition for help in battle, proclaims trust.
II.15.2-7	U	EX	Spirit of God through Azariah to Asa: 'Yahweh is with you when you are with him. And if you seek him, he will let you find him; but if you forsake him, he will forsake you' (v. 2b). Also gives an illustration (vv. 3-6).
II.16.7-9	U	EX	Hanani the seer to Asa: Yahweh will support those whose heart is his (v. 9a); gives illustrations of reliance on Syria and failure, versus reliance on Yahweh and victory.
II.19.2-3	U	EX	Jehu son of Hanani the seer to Jehoshaphat: rebuke for helping those who hate Yahweh, thus incurring wrath; praise for cultic acts and seeking God.
II.20.6-12	U	EI	prayer of Jehoshaphat before assembly: petitions God for deliverance, quotes temple petition of Solomon, expresses trust; implicit.
II.20.15-17	U	EI	Spirit of Yahweh through Jahaziel to Judah and Jehoshaphat after seeking Yahweh through prayer and fasting (vv. 3-13): because Yahweh is with them, they will be victorious.
II.20.20	U	EX	Jehoshaphat to people of Judah: 'Put your trust in Yahweh your God, and you will be established...'

II.20.37	U	EX	Eliezer the prophet to Jehoshaphat: 'Because you have allied yourself with Ahaziah, Yahweh has destroyed your works'. Making an alliance with Ahaziah was to forsake Yahweh; see II.13.4-12.
II.21.12-15	U	EX	Yahweh through letter of Elijah to Jehoram: because he had not walked in the ways of Jehoshaphat, but caused the people to play the harlot, he and the people will suffer calamity from God.
II.24.20	U	EX	Spirit of God through Zechariah to the people (including Joash): 'Because you have forsaken Yahweh, he has also forsaken you'.
II.24.22	U	EI	prayer of Zechariah (priest/prophet): petition for retribution on Joash and people for murdering him.
II.25.7-9	U	EX	dialogue between a man of God and Amaziah: if Amaziah relies on warriors hired from Israel, God will cause them to be defeated, whereas obedience will result in more than what he paid. To rely on an idolatrous nation is to forsake God; see II.13.4-12; 16.7; 19.2; 20.37; 22.3-9.
II.25.15-16	U	EX	dialogue between a prophet and Amaziah: 'I know that God has planned to destroy you, because you have done this [sought other gods (vv. 14-15)]...'
II.28.9-11	U	EI	prophet of Yahweh to army of Israel: Yahweh had caused Judah to be defeated, because he was angry with them; connected to forsaking Yahweh and other consequential military defeats (vv. 1-7).
II.29.5-11	U	EX	Hezekiah to priests and Levites: because their fathers had forsaken Yahweh and not maintained the cultus, they had suffered God's wrath.
II.30.6-9	U	EX	Hezekiah, via couriers, to all Israel and Judah: their fathers had been unfaithful to Yahweh and had received judgment, but if they return and serve Yahweh, he will be compassionate and turn to them.
II.30.18-19	U	EI	prayer of Hezekiah: petitions Yahweh to pardon the unpurified who have prepared their hearts to seek God.
II.33.7-8	S	EI	quotation of God by narrator to audience: promise of Yahweh to David and Solomon to dwell in the temple and protect Israel, if they obey the law.
II.34.23-28	B	EX	prophetess Huldah to officials of Josiah: judgment is coming on Judah, because they have forsaken Yahweh; but not during Josiah's lifetime, because he had humbled himself (second 'humbled self' is U).

Key: 1st column: location in the books of Chronicles
2nd column: U (unique material), S (synoptic), B (contains both)
3rd column: speeches without the enthymeme labeled if they contribute to character portrayal
        pos (positive character portrayal) or
        neg (negative portrayal)

I.4.9			mother to self (?): names Jabez.
I.11.1-2	S	pos	all Israel to David: affirms David as king.
I.11.5	S		Jebusites to David: reproof.
I.11.6	U		David to army (?): promise regarding first to kill a Jebusite.
I.11.17	S		David to self (?): craves water.
I.11.19	S	pos	David to three mighty men: honors mighty men.
I.12.17	U	pos	David to Benjamin and Judah: proclaims inno-cence.
I.12.18	U	pos	Amasai to David: prophetically confirms the sup-port of God and of the thirty for David.
I.13.2-3	U	pos	David to assembly of Israel: unlike Saul, he desires to bring back ark.
I.13.12	S		David to self (?): afraid to transport ark.
I.14.10	S	pos	dialogue between David and God: David inquires of God regarding battle (perhaps contrast to Saul in-tended).
I.14.11	S		David to self (?): statement about God-given victory (etymological explanation).
I.14.14-15	S	pos	God to David: answers David's inquiry regarding battle.
I.15.2	U	pos	David to self (?): instruction for only Levites to carry ark.
I.15.12-13	U	pos	David to cultic leaders: orders them to consecrate selves and carry ark, explains reason for first dis-aster.
I.16.8-36	U	pos	David to Asaph and relatives: psalm of thanksgiv-ing.
I.17.1-2	S	pos	dialogue between David and Nathan: David desires to build a house for the ark; Nathan affirms his desire.
I.19.2	S	pos	David to self (?): will show kindness to Ammonite king.
I.19.3	S		princes of Ammon to Hanun: suspicion about David.

I.19.5	S		David to humiliated messengers: to grow back beards.
I.19.12-13	S	pos	Joab to Abishai: battle plan and exhortation to be courageous, shows trust in God.
I.21.2-3	B	neg	dialogue between David and Joab: David orders census and Joab protests.
I.21.10	S		Yahweh to Gad for David: to present options of judgment to David.
I.21.11-13	B	Pos	dialogue between Gad and David: choice of judgment; David relies on God's mercy.
I.21.22-24	B	pos	dialogue between David and Ornan: David purchases site for temple altar.
I.22.1	U	pos	David to self (?): 'This is the house of Yahweh . . .'; links ch. 21 to temple concerns in chs. 22–29.
I.22.5	U	pos	David to self (?): Because Solomon is young and inexperienced, David himself will make preparations for the temple.
I.23.25-26	U	pos	David to self (?): explains division of Levites for service; since Yahweh now dwelt in Jerusalem, no need to transport tabernacle.
I.28.19	U	pos	David (?) to Solomon or self (?): Yahweh had given him understanding regarding the plan of the temple.
I.29.1-5	U	pos	David to assembly: since Solomon is young and inexperienced, David has provided for temple; they should provide in like manner.
I.29.20	U	pos	David to assembly: command to bless Yahweh.
II.2.3-10	B	pos	Solomon to Huram: to send supplies for he intends to build temple.
II.2.11-16	B	pos	Huram to Solomon: blesses Yahweh for David's wise son; makes arrangements for temple supplies.
II.5.13	U		priests and Levitical singers: praise Yahweh.
II.6.1-11	B	pos	Solomon to assembly at dedication of temple: about Yahweh's choice of Jerusalem, David's intentions, promise of Davidic dynasty, and building of temple.
II.7.3	U		sons of Israel: praise Yahweh for everlasting love.
II.8.11	U	pos	Solomon to self (?): that his wife, Pharaoh's daughter, would have a separate house for reasons of cultic purity.
II.9.5-8	S	pos	queen of Sheba to Solomon: praises him and blesses Yahweh for 'establishing' (U) Israel.
II.10.4-16	S	neg	dialogue among all Israel, Rehoboam, the elders, and the young advisors: over levy of work; the Chronicler's main cause for the division of the kingdom.
II.11.3	S		word of Yahweh to Shemaiah for Rehoboam: not to fight Jeroboam.

II.12.6	U	pos	Rehoboam and princes to themselves (?) in response to word of judgment: 'Yahweh is righteous'.
II.16.3	S	neg	Asa to Ben-hadad: offer to pay for help against Northern Kingdom.
II.18.3-33	S	pos	dialogue among Jehoshaphat, Ahab, court prophets, messenger and Micaiah: regarding battle; Jehoshaphat wants to inquire from a prophet of Yahweh.
II.19.6-7	U	pos	Jehoshaphat to judges: to judge for Yahweh, showing fear of Yahweh and show no partiality.
II.19.9-11	U	pos	Jehoshaphat to judges: to fear Yahweh and to warn the people; appoints officials.
II.20.2	U		people to Jehoshaphat: enemies coming.
II.20.21	U		singers in front of the army: praise Yahweh's everlasting love.
II.23.3-7	B	pos	priest Jehoiada to assembly: to overthrow Athaliah and to restore Davidic dynasty promised by Yahweh.
II.23.13	S		Athaliah to mob: 'Treason!'
II.23.14	S	pos	priest Jehoiada to captains of army: for Athaliah to be put to death; concerned with cultic purity.
II.24.5	U	pos	Joash to priests and Levites: to collect money and repair temple (U wording, but S tradition).
II.24.6	U	pos	Joash to chief priest Jehoiada: rebuke for not requiring Levites to bring in the money commanded (U wording, but S tradition).
II.25.17-19	S	neg	dialogue between Amaziah of Judah and Joash of Israel: challenged to battle and taunting fable in reply.
II.28.13	U		heads of Ephraim to army of Israel: command not to bring captives from Judah.
II.28.23	U	neg	Ahaz to self (?): why he sacrificed to gods of Damascus (U statement in synoptic section).
II.29.18-19	U	pos	priests and Levites to Hezekiah: report back that they carried out his command to consecrate temple (vv. 5-11).
II.29.31	U	pos	Hezekiah to priests and Levites: command to offer sacrifices.
II.31.10	U	pos	chief priest Azariah to Hezekiah: about surplus contributions; show positive response to Hezekiah's cultic efforts (v. 4).
II.32.4	U		people to selves (?): they stopped up water supply because the Assyrians were coming.
II.32.7-8	U	pos	Hezekiah to military officers: to be courageous and not fear Assyrians, that Yahweh is their help.

II.32.10-15	U		messengers of Sennacherib to Jerusalem: not to trust Hezekiah or Yahweh (U wording in S tradition).
II.32.17	U		letters of Sennacherib to Jerusalem: the God of Hezekiah will not deliver them.
II.33.4	S		quotation of Yahweh by narrator to audience: promise of Yahweh to dwell in Jerusalem forever.
II.34.15	S		Hilkiah the priest to Shaphan the scribe: found the book of the law.
II.34.16-18	B		Shaphan to Josiah: carried out his orders, found book of the law.
II.34.21	S	pos	Josiah to officials: to inquire of Yahweh, through Huldah the prophetess, about the book of the law.
II.35.3-6	U	pos	Josiah to Levites: place ark in temple, prepare themselves, slaughter Passover animals for the people.
II.35.21	U		Neco, via messengers, to Josiah: not to fight against him, for God is with him; a message 'from the mouth of God' (v. 22) (U statement in S tradition).
II.35.23	U		Josiah to servants: that he was wounded.
II.36.23	U		edict from Cyrus to people in exile: Yahweh had appointed him to build the temple and to allow the people to return (parallel to Ezra 1.2-3a).

LIST 4: DIVINE SPEECH MATERIAL

Key: 1st column: location in the books of Chronicles
2nd column: U (unique material), S (synoptic), B (contains both)
3rd column: speeches with the enthymeme labeled either EI
(enthymeme implicit) or EX (enthymeme explicit)
speeches without the enthymeme labeled if they contribute to character portrayal
pos (positive character portrayal) or
neg (negative portrayal)

I.14.10	S	pos	dialogue between David and God: David inquires of God regarding battle (perhaps contrast to Saul intended).
I.14.14-15	S	pos	God to David: answers David's inquiry regarding battle.
I.17.4-14	B	EI	God to Nathan for David: God's promise to establish Davidic dynasty in response to David's desire to build temple.
I.21.10	S		Yahweh to Gad for David: to present options of judgment to David.
II.1.7-12	B	EI	dialogue between Solomon and Yahweh after Solomon had sacrificed to Yahweh: connection between seeking and the promised wisdom, wealth, and honor is implicit.
II.7.12-22	B	EX	Yahweh to Solomon: U section (vv. 13-15) states enthymeme in terms of 'humbling selves', 'seeking', and 'turning'; promises continuity of dynasty on condition of walking as David walked (vv. 17-18); states negative side of forsaking as well (vv. 19-22).
II.33.4	S		quotation of Yahweh by narrator to audience: promise of Yahweh to dwell in Jerusalem forever.
II.33.7-8	S	EI	quotation of God by narrator to audience: promise of Yahweh to David and Solomon to dwell in the temple and protect Israel, if they obey the law.

LIST 5: ROYAL PRAYERS

Key: 1st column: location in the books of Chronicles
2nd column: U (unique material), S (synoptic), B (contains both)
3rd column: speeches with the enthymeme labeled either EI
(enthymeme implicit) or EX (enthymeme explicit)
speeches without the enthymeme labeled if they contribute to character portrayal
pos (positive character portrayal) or
neg (negative portrayal).

I.17.16-27	B	EI	prayer of David in response to divine promise: connection between Yahweh establishing David and David establishing Yahweh (vv. 23-24).
I.21.8	S	EI	prayer of David in response to judgment: confession of sin and request for iniquity to be removed.
I.21.17	B	EI	prayer of David in response to pestilence: accepts responsibility for sin and petitions God to spare the people.
I.29.10-19	U	EI	praise and prayer of David: defines further the signs of blessing: power, victory, riches, honor (vv. 11-12), connection to building temple (v. 16) seeking (v. 17) and obedience (v. 18).
II.6.14-42	B	EI	(S with U addition of vv. 40-42) Solomon's prayer of dedication: requests Yahweh's favorable response when people turn to God in need.
II.14.11	U	EI	prayer of Asa: petition for help in battle, proclaims trust.
II.20.6-12	U	EI	prayer of Jehoshaphat before asembly: petitions God for deliverance, quotes temple petition of Solomon, expresses trust; implicit.
II.24.22	U	EI	prayer of Zechariah (priest/ prophet); petition for retribution on Joash and people for murdering him.
II.30.18-19	U	EI	prayer of Hezekiah: petitions Yahweh to pardon the unpurified who have prepared their hearts to seek God.

LIST 6: ROYAL SPEECHES

Key: 1st column: location in the books of Chronicles
         2nd column: U (unique material), S (synoptic), B (contains both)
         3rd column: speeches with the enthymeme labeled either EI
         (enthymeme implicit) or EX (enthymeme explicit)
         speeches without the enthymeme labeled if they contribute to char-
         acter portrayal
              pos (positive character portrayal) or
              neg (negative portrayal)

I.12.17	U	pos	David to Benjamin and Judah: proclaims innocence.
I.13.2-3	U	pos	David to assembly of Israel: unlike Saul, he desires to bring back ark.
I.22.7-16	U	EI	David's charge to Solomon: repeats God's promise, 'He shall build a house for my name... and I will establish the throne of his kingdom...'
I.22.18-19	U	EI	David's charge to the leaders: Yahweh has given rest, therefore seek Yahweh, build the temple; causal relationship implicit, defines further the nature of seeking.
I.28.2-8	U	EX	David to leaders: makes explicit the relationship of blessing to obedience (v. 7) and seeking to blessing (v. 8).
I.28.9-10	U	EX	David to Solomon: 'If you seek him, he will let you find him; but if you forsake him, he will reject you forever'. Positive and negative sides of enthymeme stated with 'seeking' connected to the cult (v. 10).
I.28.20-21	U	EI	David to Solomon: connection between Yahweh's presence and the establishment of the cult.
I.29.1-5	U	pos	David to assembly: since Solomon is young and inexperienced, David has provided for temple; they should provide in like manner.
II.2.3-10	B	pos	Solomon to Huram: to send supplies for he intends to build temple.
II.2.11-16	B	pos	Huram to Solomon: blesses Yahweh for David's wise son; makes arrangements for temple supplies.
II.6.1-11	B	pos	Solomon to assembly at dedication of temple: about Yahweh's choice of Jerusalem, David's intentions, promise of Davidic dynasty, and building of temple.
II.9.5-8	S	pos	Queen of Sheba to Solomon: praises him and blesses Yahweh for 'establishing' (U) Israel.

II.13.4-12	U	EI	King Abijah to Jeroboam and Israel: rebukes them for rebelling against the Davidic dynasty and for forsaking Yahweh, warns them of failure.
II.14.7	U	EI	Asa to Judah: 'The land is before us, because we have sought Yahweh our God...'
II.19.6-7	U	pos	Jehoshaphat to judges: to judge for Yahweh, showing fear of Yahweh and no partiality.
II.19.9-11	U	pos	Jehoshaphat to judges: to fear Yahweh and to warn the people; appoints officials.
II.20.20	U	EX	Jehoshaphat to people of Judah: 'Put your trust in Yahweh your God, and you will be established...'
II.29.5-11	U	EX	Hezekiah to priests and Levites: because their fathers had forsaken Yahweh and not maintained the cultus, they had suffered God's wrath.
II.30.6-9	U	EX	Hezekiah, via couriers, to all Israel and Judah: their fathers had been unfaithful to Yahweh and had received judgment, but if they return and serve Yahweh, he will be compassionate and turn to them.
II.32.7-8	U	pos	Hezekiah to military officers: to be courageous and not fear Assyrians, that Yahweh is their help.
II.35.3-6	U	pos	Josiah to Levites: place ark in temple, prepare themselves, slaughter Passover animals for the people.

Key: 1st column: location in the books of Chronicles
         2nd column: U (unique material), S (synoptic), B (contains both)
         3rd column: speeches with the enthymeme labeled either EI
         (enthymeme implicit) or EX (enthymem explicit)
         speeches without the enthymeme labeled if they contribute to char-
         acter portrayal
                  pos (positive character portrayal) or
                  neg (negative portrayal).

I.11.6	U		David to army (?): promise regarding first to kill a Jebusite.
I.11.17	S		David to self (?): craves water.
I.11.19	S	pos	David to three mighty men: honors mighty men.
I.13.12	S		David to self (?): afraid to transport ark.
I.14.11	S		David to self (?): statement about God-given victory (etymological explanation).
I.15.2	U	pos	David to self (?): instruction for only Levites to carry ark.
I.15.12-13	U	pos	David to cultic leaders: orders them to consecrate selves and carry ark, explains reason for first disaster.
I.16.8-36	U	pos	David to Asaph and relatives: psalm of thanksgiving.
I.19.2	S	pos	David to self (?): will show kindness to Ammonite king.
I.22.1	U	pos	David to self (?): 'This is the house of Yahweh . . .'; links ch. 21 to temple concerns in chs. 22–29.
I.22.5	U	pos	David to self (?): Because Solomon is young and inexperienced, David himself will make preparations for the temple.
I.23.25-26	U	pos	David to self (?): explains division of Levites for service; since Yahweh now dwelt in Jerusalem, no need to transport tabernacle.
I.28.19	U	pos	David (?) to Solomon or self (?): Yahweh had given him understanding regarding the plan of the temple.
I.29.20	U	pos	David to assembly: command to bless Yahweh.
II.8.11	U	pos	Solomon to self (?): that his wife, Pharaoh's daughter, would have a separate house for reasons of cultic purity.

II.12.6	U	pos	Rehoboam and princes to themselves (?) in response to word of judgment: 'Yahweh is righteous'.
II.16.3	S	neg	Asa to Ben-hadad: offer to pay for help against Northern Kingdom.
II.24.5	U	pos	Joash to priests and Levites: to collect money and repair temple (U wording, but S tradition).
II.24.6	U	pos	Joash to chief priest Jehoiada: rebuke for not requiring Levites to bring in the money commanded (U wording, but S tradition).
II.28.23	U	neg	Ahaz to self (?): why he sacrificed to gods of Damascus (U statement in synoptic section).
II.29.31	U	pos	Hezekiah to priests and Levites: command to offer sacrifices.
II.34.21	S	pos	Josiah to officials: to inquire of Yahweh, through Huldah the prophetess, about the book of the law.
II.35.21	U		Neco, via messengers, to Josiah: not to fight against him, for God is with him; a message 'from the mouth of God' (v. 22) (U statement in S tradition).
II.35.23	U		Josiah to servants: that he was wounded.
II.36.23	U		edict from Cyrus to people in exile: Yahweh had appointed him to build the temple and to allow the people to return (parallel to Ezra 1.2-3a).

LIST 8: PROPHETIC SPEECH MATERIAL

Key: 1st column: location in the books of Chronicles
2nd column: U (unique material), S (synoptic), B (contains both)
3rd column: speeches with the enthymeme labeled either EI
(enthymeme implicit) or EX (enthymeme explicit)
speeches without the enthymeme labeled if they contribute to character portrayal
        pos (positive character portrayal) or
        neg (negative portrayal)

I.12.18	U	pos	Amasai to David: prophetically confirms the support of God and of the thirty for David.
I.17.1-2	S	pos	dialogue between David and Nathan: David desires to build a house for the ark; Nathan affirms his desire.
I.21.11-13	B	pos	dialogue between Gad and David: choice of judgment; David relies on God's mercy.
II.11.3	S		word of Yahweh to Shemaiah for Rehoboam: not to fight Jeroboam.
II.12.5	U	EX	Shemaiah to Rehoboam (word of Yahweh): 'You have forsaken me, so even I have forsaken you into the hand of Shishak'.
II.12.7-8	U	EX	word of Yahweh through Shemaiah: because Rehoboam and the leaders humbled themselves, God will grant a partial deliverance.
II.15.2-7	U	EX	Spirit of God through Azariah to Asa: 'Yahweh is with you when you are with him. And if you seek him, he will let you find him; but if you forsake him, he will forsake you' (v. 2b). Also gives an illustration (vv. 3-6).
II.16.7-9	U	EX	Hanani the seer to Asa: Yahweh will support those whose heart is his (v. 9a); gives illustrations of reliance on Syria and failure, versus reliance on Yahweh and victory.
II.19.2-3	U	EX	Jehu son of Hanani the seer to Jehoshaphat: rebuke for helping those who hate Yahweh, thus incurring wrath; praise for cultic acts and seeking God.
II.20.15-17	U	EI	Spirit of Yahweh through Jahaziel to Judah and Jehoshaphat after seeking Yahweh through prayer and fasting (vv. 3-13): because Yahweh is with them, they will be victorious.

II.20.37	U	Ex	Eliezer the prophet to Jehoshaphat: 'Because you have allied yourself with Ahaziah, Yahweh has destroyed your works'. Making an alliance with Ahaziah was to forsake Yahweh; see II.13.4-12.
II.21.12-15	U	EX	Yahweh through letter of Elijah to Jehoram: because he had not walked in the ways of Jehoshaphat, but caused the people to play the harlot, he and the people will suffer calamity from God.
II.24.20	U	EX	Spirit of God through Zechariah to the people (including Joash): 'Because you have forsaken Yahweh, he has also forsaken you'.
II.25.7-9	U	EX	dialogue between a man of God and Amaziah: if Amaziah relies on warriors hired from Israel, God will cause them to be defeated, whereas obedience will result in more than what he paid. To rely on an idolatrous nation is to forsake God, see II.13.4-12; 16.7; 19.2; 20.37; 22.3-9.
II.25.15-16	U	EX	dialogue between a prophet and Amaziah: 'I know that God has planned to destroy you, because you have done this [sought other gods] (vv. 14-15) . . .'
II.28.9-11	U	EI	prophet of Yahweh to army of Israel: Yahweh had caused Judah to be defeated, because he was angry with them; connected to forsaking Yahweh and other consequential military defeats (vv. 1-7).
II.34.23-28	B	EX	prophetess Huldah to officials of Josiah: judgment is coming on Judah, because they have forsaken Yahweh; but not during Josiah's lifetime, because he had humbled himself (second 'humbled self' is U).
II.35.21	U		Neco, via messengers, to Josiah: not to fight against him, for God is with him; a message 'from the mouth of God' (v. 22) (U statement in S tradition).

BIBLIOGRAPHY

Ackroyd, P.R. 'The Chronicler as Exegete', *JSOT* 2 (1977), pp. 2-32.
—'Chronicles, I and II', *IDBSup*. Ed. K. Crim *et al*. Nashville: Abingdon, 1976, pp. 156-58.
—'The Historical Literature', *The Hebrew Bible and its Modern Interpreters*. Ed. D.A. Knight and G.M. Tucker. Philadelphia: Fortress, 1985, pp. 297-323.
—'The Theology of the Chronicler', *Lexington Theological Quarterly* 8 (1973), pp. 101-16.
Albright, W.F. 'The Date and Personality of the Chronicler', *JBL* 40 (1921), pp. 104-24.
—'The Judicial Reform of Jehoshaphat', *Alexander Marx Jubilee Volume*. New York: Jewish Theological Seminary of America, 1950, pp. 61-82.
Allen, L.C. *The Greek Chronicles: The Relation of the Septuagint of I and II Chronicles to the Massoretic Text*. 2 vols. VTSup, 25, 27. Leiden: Brill, 1974. Vol. 2: *Textual Criticism*.
—'Kerygmatic Units in 1 & 2 Chronicles', *JSOT* 41 (1988), pp. 21-36.
Alter, R. *The Art of Biblical Narrative*. New York: Basic Books, 1981.
Aristotle, *The Basic Works of Aristotle*. Ed. R. McKeon. New York: Random House, 1941; *Rhetorica*, trans. W. Rhys Roberts.
Arnhart, L. *Aristotle on Political Reasoning*. DeKalb: Northern Illinois University, 1981.
Baldwin, C.S. *Ancient Rhetoric and Poetic*. New York: Macmillan, 1924.
Barnes, W.E. 'The Midrashic Element in Chronicles', *Expositor*, fifth series, 4 (1896), pp. 426-39.
Beecher, W.J. 'Chronicles, Books of', *The International Standard Bible Encyclopaedia*. 5 vols. Ed. James Orr *et al*. Chicago: Howard-Severance, 1915, 1.629-35.
Berlin, A. *Poetics and Interpretation of Biblical Narrative*. Sheffield: Almond, 1983.
Beyer, G. 'Beiträge zur Territorialgeschichte von Südwestpalästina im Altertum', *ZDPV* 54 (1931), pp. 113-70.
Bloch, R. 'Midrash', *Approaches to Ancient Judaism: Theory and Practice*. Ed. W.S. Green. Brown Judaic Studies, 1. Missoula: Scholars, 1978, pp. 29-50.
Braun, R.L. 'The Significance of 1 Chronicles 22, 28, and 29 for the Structure and Theology of the Work of the Chronicler.' Th.D. dissertation. Concordia Seminary, 1971.
—'Solomon, the Chosen Temple Builder: The Significance of 1 Chronicles 22, 28, and 29 for the Theology of Chronicles', *JBL* 95 (1976), pp. 581-90.
—'Solomonic Apologetic in Chronicles', *JBL* 92 (1973), pp. 503-16.
Bright, J. *A History of Israel*. Philadelphia: Westminster, 1959.

Bruner, E.M. 'Ethnography as Narrative', *The Anthropology of Experience*. Ed. V. Turner and E.M. Bruner; Urbana: University of Illinois, 1986, pp. 139-55.

Chang, W.I. 'The *Tendenz* of the Chronicler.' Ph.D. dissertation. Hartford Seminary Foundation, 1973.

Cheyne, T.K. *The Decline and Fall of the Kingdom of Judah*. London: A. & C. Black, 1908.

Childs, B.S. *Introduction to the Old Testament as Scripture*. Philadelphia: Fortress, 1979.

Clements, R.E. *One Hundred Years of Old Testament Interpretation*. Philadelphia: Westminster, 1976.

Cogan, M. 'The Chronicler's Use of Chronology as Illuminated by Neo-Assyrian Royal Inscriptions.' *Empirical Models for Biblical Criticism*. Ed. J.H. Tigay. Philadelphia: University of Pennsylvania, 1985, pp. 197-209.

Colenso, J.W. *The Pentateuch and the Book of Joshua Critically Examined*. 5 vols. London: Longman, Green, Longman, Robert & Green, 1862-79.

Conley, T. '*Pathe* and *Pisteis*: Aristotle, "Rhetoric", II, 2-11', *Hermes* 110/3 (1982), pp. 300-15.

Corbett, E.P.J. *Classical Rhetoric for the Modern Student*. New York: Oxford University, 1965.

Cross, F.M. 'A Reconstruction of the Judean Restoration', *JBL* 94 (1975), pp. 4-18.

Curtis E.L., and A.A. Madsen. *A Critical and Exegetical Commentary on the Books of Chronicles*. ICC. New York: Charles Scribner's Sons, 1910.

De Vries, S.J. *1 and 2 Chronicles*. The Forms of the Old Testament Literature, 11. Grand Rapids: Eerdmans, 1989.

Dibelius, M. 'The Speeches in Acts and Ancient Historiography', *Studies in the Acts of the Apostles*. Ed. H. Greeven. Trans. M. Ling. New York: Scribner's, 1956, pp. 138-85.

Dillard, R.B. 'The Chronicler's Solomon', *WTJ* 43 (1980), pp. 289-300.

—'The Literary Structure of the Chronicler's Solomon Narrative', *JSOT* 30 (1984), pp. 85-93.

—'Reward and Punishment in Chronicles: The Theology of Immediate Retribution', *WTJ* 46 (1984), pp. 164-72.

Driver, S.R. 'Hebrew Authority', *Authority and Archaeology: Sacred and Profane*. Ed. David G. Hogarth. New York: Charles Scribner's Sons, 1899, pp. 1-152.

—*An Introduction to the Literature of the Old Testament*. 9th edn. Edinburgh: T. & T. Clark, 1913.

—'The Speeches in Chronicles', *The Expositor*, fifth series, 1 (1895), pp. 241-56 and 2 (1895), pp. 286-308.

Eichhorn, G.J. *Einleitung in das Alte Testament*. 3 vols. 3rd edn. Leipzig: Weidman, 1803.

Eissfeldt, O. *The Old Testament: An Introduction*. Trans. of 3rd edn of 1964 by P.R. Ackroyd. Oxford: Basil Blackwell, 1965; New York: Harper & Row, 1976.

Engler, H. 'The Attitude of the Chronicler toward the Davidic Monarchy.' Th.D. dissertation. Union Theological Seminary in Virginia, 1967.

Fishbane, M. *Biblical Interpretation in Ancient Israel*. Oxford: Clarendon, 1985.

Freedman, D.N. 'The Chronicler's Purpose', *CBQ* 23 (1961), pp. 436-42.

French, V. 'The Speeches in Chronicles: A Reply', *The Expositor*, fifth series, 2 (1895), pp. 140-52.

Galling, K. *Die Bücher der Chronik, Esra, Nehemia*. Das Alte Testament Deutsch, 12. Göttingen: Vandenhoeck & Ruprecht, 1954.

Gesenius, W. *Geschichte der hebräischen Sprache und Schrift: Eine philologisch-historische Einleitung in die Sprachlehren und Wörterbücher der hebräischen Sprache*. Leipzig: Friedrich Christian Wilhelm Vogel, 1815; reprint edn, Hildesheim: Georg Olms, 1973.

Gibson, W. 'Authors, Speakers, Readers, and Mock Reader', *Reader-Response Criticism: From Formalism to Post-Structuralism*. Ed. J.P. Tompkins. Baltimore: Johns Hopkins University, 1980, pp. 1-6.

Gitay, Y. 'Rhetorical Analysis of Isaiah 40–48: A Study of the Art of Persuasion.' Ph.D. dissertation. Emory University, 1978.

Graf, K.H. *Die geschichtlichen Bücher des Alten Testaments*. Leipzig: T.O. Weigel, 1866.

Graham, M.P. 'The Utilization of 1 and 2 Chronicles in the Reconstruction of the Israelite History in the Nineteenth Century.' Ph.D. dissertation. Emory University, 1983.

Gramberg, K.P.W. *Die Chronik*. Halle: Eduard Anton, 1823.

Gray, G.B. *A Critical Introduction to the Old Testament*. New York: Charles Scribner's Sons, 1913.

Grimaldi, W. *Aristotle, Rhetoric I: A Commentary*. Bronx, NY: Fordham University, 1980.

Haevernick, H.A.C. *Handbuch der historisch-kritischen Einleitung in das Alte Testament*. 3 vols. Erlangen: Cark Heyder, 1839.

Hernadi, P. 'Clio's Cousins: Historiography as Translation, Fiction, and Criticism', *New Literary History* 7 (1976), pp. 245-57.

Im, Tae-Soo. *Das Davidbild in den Chronikbüchern: David als Idealbild des theokratischen Messianismus für den Chronisten*. Europäische Hochschulschriften XXIII/263. Frankfurt am Main: Peter Lang, 1985.

Japhet, S. 'The Historical Reliability of Chronicles: The History of the Problem and its Place in Biblical Research', *JSOT* 33 (1985), pp. 83-107.

—'The Ideology of the Book of Chronicles and its Place in Biblical Thought' (Hebrew). Ph.D. dissertation. Jerusalem: Hebrew University, 1973. English Abstract, pp. v-xxxviii.

—'The Supposed Common Authorship of Chronicles and Ezra–Nehemiah Investigated Anew', *VT* 18 (1968), pp. 330-71.

Johnstone, W. 'Guilt and Atonement: The Theme of 1 and 2 Chronicles', *A Word in Season: Essays in Honor of William McKane*. Ed. J.D. Martin and P.R. Davies. JSOTSup, 42. Sheffield: JSOT, 1986, pp. 113-38.

Kapelrud, A.S. 'Temple Building, a Task for Gods and Kings', *Or* 32 (1963), pp. 56-62.

Keil, C.F. *Apologetischer Versuch über die Bücher der Chronik und über die Integrität des Buches Esra*. Berlin: Ludwig Oehmigke, 1833.

Keil, C.F. and F.J. Delitzsch, *Biblical Commentary on the Old Testament*. 25 vols. Clark's Foreign Theological Library, fourth series. Edinburgh: T. & T. Clark, 1878; reprint edn Grand Rapids: Eerdmans, 1978. Vol. 7: *The Books of the Chronicles* by C.F. Keil.

Kennedy, G. *The Art of Persuasion in Greece*. Princeton: Princeton University, 1963.

—*Classical Rhetoric and its Christian and Secular Tradition from Ancient to Modern Times*. Chapel Hill: University of North Carolina, 1980.

—*New Testament Interpretation through Rhetorical Criticism.* Chapel Hill: University of North Carolina, 1984.

Klein, R.W. 'Historical Allusions Within the Genealogies'. Paper presented at the Annual Meeting of the Society of Biblical Literature, Anaheim, November, 1985.

Lemke, W.E. 'Synoptic Studies in the Chronicler's History.' Th.D. thesis. Harvard Divinity School, 1963.

Macalister, R.A.S. 'The Craftsmen's Guild of the Tribe of Judah', *PEQ* 37 (1905), pp. 243-53, 328-42.

McFadyen, J.E. *Introduction to the Old Testament.* London: Hodder & Stoughton, 1932.

McKenzie, S.L. 'The Chronicler's Use of the Deuteronomistic History.' Th.D. dissertation. Harvard Divinity School, 1983.

Macy, H.R. 'The Sources of the Books of Chronicles: A Reassessment.' Ph.D. dissertation. Harvard University, 1975.

Meyer, E. *Die Entstehung des Judenthums.* Halle: Max Niemeyer, 1896.

Micheel, R. *Die Seher- und Prophetenüberlieferungen in der Chronik.* BET, 18. Frankfurt am Main: Peter Lang, 1983.

Mink, L.O. 'History and Fiction as Modes of Comprehending', *New Literary Inquiry* 1 (1969/70), pp. 541-58.

Moriarty, F.L. 'The Chronicler's Account of Hezekiah's Reform', *CBQ* 27 (1965), pp. 399-406.

Mosis, R. *Untersuchungen zur Theologie des chronistischen Geschichtswerkes.* FTS, 92. Freiburg: Herder, 1973.

Movers, F.K. *Kritische Untersuchungen über die biblische Chronik.* Bonn: T. Habricht, 1834.

Myers, J.M. *I and II Chronicles.* Anchor Bible. Garden City, NY: Doubleday, 1965.

—'The Kerygma of the Chronicler: History and Theology in the Service of Religion', *Int* 20 (1966), pp. 259-73.

Newsome, Jr, J.D. 'The Chronicler's View of Prophecy.' Ph.D. dissertation. Vanderbilt University, 1973.

North, R. 'Does Archeology Prove Chronicles' Sources?', *A Light unto My Path: Old Testament Studies in Honor of Jacob Myers.* Ed. H.N. Bream, R.D. Heim, and C.A. Moore. Philadelphia: Temple University, 1974, pp. 375-401.

—'Theology of the Chronicler', *JBL* 82 (1963), pp. 369-81.

Noth, M. 'Eine siedlungsgeographische Liste in 1. Chr. 2 und 4', *ZDPV* 55 (1932), pp. 97-124.

—*Überlieferungsgeschichtliche Studien.* Wiesbaden-Biebrich: Becker, 1943; reprint edn, Tübingen: Max Niemeyer, 1957.

Oesterley, W.O.E., and T.H. Robinson, *An Introduction to the Books of the Old Testament.* London: SPCK, 1934; Cleveland: World, 1958.

Osborne, W.L. 'The Genealogies of 1 Chronicles 1–9.' Ph.D. dissertation. The Dropsie University, 1979.

Patte, D. *Early Jewish Hermeneutic in Palestine.* SBLDS, 22. Missoula: Scholars, 1975.

Payne, J.B. 'I Chronicles, II Chronicles', *The Wycliffe Bible Commentary.* Ed. C.F. Pfeiffer and E.F. Harrison. London: Oliphants, 1962.

Petersen, N.R. 'Literary Criticism in Biblical Studies', *Orientation by Disorientation: Studies in Literary Criticism and Biblical Literary Criticism. In honor of W.A. Beardslee*. Ed. R.A. Spencer. Pittsburgh: Pickwick, 1980, pp. 25-50.

Pfeiffer, R.H. *Introduction to the Old Testament*. 2nd edn. New York: Harper & Brothers, 1948.

Prince, G. 'Introduction to the Study of the Narratee', *Reader-Response Criticism: From Formalism to Post-Structuralism*. Ed. J.P. Tompkins. Baltimore: Johns Hopkins University, 1980, pp. 7-25.

Rad, G. von. *Das Geschichtsbild des chronistischen Werkes*. BWANT, 54. Stuttgart: W. Kohlhammer, 1930.

—'The Levitical Sermon in I and II Chronicles', *The Problem of the Hexateuch and Other Essays*. New York: McGraw-Hill, 1966, pp. 267-80.

—*Old Testament Theology*. 2 vols. Trans. D.M.G. Stalker. New York: Harper & Row, 1962, 1965.

Rawlinson, G. *Ezra and Nehemiah: Their Lives and Times*. Men of the Bible. New York: Fleming H. Revell, 1890.

—*The Historical Evidences of the Truth of the Scripture Records, Stated Anew, with Special Reference to the Doubts and Discoveries of Modern Times*. Bampton Lecture, 1859. London: John Murray, 1859.

Ricoeur, P. 'The Narrative Function', *Semeia* 13 (1978), pp. 177-202.

Rigsby, R.O. 'The Historiography of Speeches and Prayers in the Books of Chronicles.' Th.D. dissertation. Southern Baptist Theological Seminary, 1973.

Rothstein, J.W. and J. Haenel. *Kommentar zum ersten Buch der Chronik*. 2 parts. KAT, 18. Leipzig: A. Deichert, 1927.

Rudolph, W. *Chronikbücher*. HAT, 21. Tübingen: J.C.B. Mohr (Paul Siebeck), 1955.

—'Problems of the Books of Chronicles', *VT* 4 (1954), pp. 401-409.

Ryan, E.E. *Aristotle's Theory of Rhetorical Argumentation*. Montreal: Bellarmin, 1984.

Robbins, V. 'Rhetorical Arguments in Galatians 5–6.' Paper presented at Emory University, October 1985.

Sayce, A.H. *Fresh Light from the Ancient Monuments*. By-Paths of Bible Knowledge 3 (later changed to 2). London: The Religious Tract Society, 1883.

—*The 'Higher Criticism' and the Verdict of the Monuments*. 2nd edn. London: SPCK, 1894 [1893].

Schaefer, G.E. 'The Significance of Seeking God in the Purpose of the Chronicler.' Th.D. dissertation. Southern Baptist Theological Seminary, 1972.

Scholes R. and R. Kellogg, *The Nature of Narrative*. Oxford: Oxford University Press, 1966.

Schraeder, E. *The Cuneiform Inscriptions and the Old Testament*. 2 vols. Trans. from 2nd edn by O.C. Whitehouse. London: Williams and Norgate, 1885, 1888.

Smith, W.R. *The Old Testament in the Jewish Church: A Course of Lectures on Biblical Criticism*. 2nd edn. London: A. & C. Black, 1892; reprint edn, 1908.

Soares, T.G. 'The Import of the Chronicles as a Piece of Religio-Historical Literature', *American Journal of Theology* 3 (1899), pp. 251-74.

Spinoza, B. de. *The Chief Works of Benedict de Spinoza*. Trans. R.H.M. Elwes. Vol. 1: *Theologico-Political Treatise*. George Bell & Sons, 1883; reprint edn, New York: Dover, 1951.

Spiro, A. 'Manners of Rewriting Biblical History from Chronicles to Pseudo-Philo.' Ph.D. dissertation. Columbia University, 1953.

Talmon, S. 'Divergences in the Calendar Reckoning in Ephraim and Judah', *VT* 8 (1958), pp. 48-74.

—'1 and 2 Chronicles', *The Literary Guide to the Bible*. Ed. R. Alter and F. Kermode. Cambridge, MA: Belknap Press of Harvard University, 1987, pp. 365-72.

Throntveit, M.A. *When Kings Speak: Royal Speech and Royal Prayer in Chronicles*. SBLDS, 93. Atlanta: Scholars, 1987.

Thucydides. *The History of the Peloponnesian War*. Trans. R. Crawley. Rev. by R. Feetham. *Great Books of the Western World*. Ed. R.M. Hutchins. Vol. 6. London: William Benton for Encyclopaedia Britannica, 1952.

Torrey, C.C. *The Chronicler's History of Israel: Chronicles–Ezra–Nehemiah Restored to its Original Form*. New Haven: Yale University, 1954.

—*The Composition and Historical Value of Ezra–Nehemiah*. Giessen: J. Ricker, 1896.

—*Ezra Studies*. Chicago: University of Chicago, 1910.

Turner, V. *Dramas, Fields, and Metaphors: Symbolic Action in Human Society*. Ithaca: Cornell University, 1974.

Van Seters, J. *In Search of History: Historiography in the Ancient World and the Origins of Biblical History*. New Haven: Yale University, 1983.

Vatke, W. *Historisch-kritische Einleitung in des Alte Testament*. Ed. H.G.S. Preiss. Bonn: Emil Strauss, 1886.

Welch, A.C. *The Work of the Chronicler: Its Purpose and Date*. London: Oxford University Press, 1939.

Wellhausen, J. *Prolegomena to the History of Ancient Israel*. Trans. of 2nd edn of 1883 by A. Menzies and J.S. Black. Edinburgh: A. & C. Black, 1885; reprint edn, Cleveland: World, 1957.

Welten, P. *Geschichte und Geschichtsdarstellung in den Chronikbüchern* (WMANT, 42: Neukirchen-Vluyn: Neukirchener Verlag, 1973.

Westermann, C. *Basic Forms of Prophetic Speech*. Trans. H.C. White. London: Lutterworth, 1967.

Wette, W.M.L. de. *Beiträge zur Einleitung in das Alte Testament*. 2 vols. Halle: Schimmelpfennig, vol. 1, 1806, vol. 2, 1807.

White, H. *Metahistory: The Historical Imagination in Nineteenth-Century Europe*. Baltimore: The Johns Hopkins University, 1973.

—'The Value of Narrativity in the Representation of Reality', *Critical Inquiry* 7 (1980), pp. 5-27.

—'Rhetoric and History', *Theories of History*. Ed. H. White and F.E. Manuel. Los Angeles: University of California, 1978, pp. 3-24.

Winckler, H. 'Bemerkungen zur Chronik als Geschichtsquelle', *Alttestamentliche Untersuchungen*. Leipzig: Eduard Pfeiffer, 1892.

Willi, T. *Die Chronik als Auslegung: Untersuchungen zur literarischen Gestaltung der historischen Überlieferung Israels*. FRLANT, 106. Göttingen: Vandenhoeck & Ruprecht, 1972.

Williamson, H.G.M. 'The Accession of Solomon in the Books of Chronicles', *VT* 26 (1976), pp. 351-61.

—*1 and 2 Chronicles*. New Century Bible Commentary. Grand Rapids, MI: Eerdmans, 1982.

—*Israel in the Books of Chronicles*. Cambridge: Cambridge University Press, 1977.

—' "We are yours, O David": The Setting and Purpose of 1 Chronicles xii 1-23', *Remembering All the Way*. OTS, 21. Leiden: Brill, 1981.

Young, E.J. *An Introduction to the Old Testament*. Grand Rapids, MI: Eerdmans, 1949; reset edn, 1958.

Zunz, L. *Die gottesdienstlichen Vorträge der Juden historisch entwickelt: Ein Beitrag zur Altertumskunde und biblischen Kritik, zur Literatur- und Religionsgeschichte*. Reprint edn, Hildesheim: Georg Olms, 1966.

INDEXES

INDEX OF BIBLICAL REFERENCES

22.9	60	28.9b	101	1.7-12	123, 160,
22.10	59	28.10	61, 159,		167
22.11-13	60, 101		171	1.11-12	79n
22.13	66, 142	28.11-19	62, 142	1.14-17	63, 64
22.14	59	28.19	130n,	1.14	78
22.18-19	101, 159,		131, 164,	2-8	63
	171		173	2	63
22.18	78	28.20-21	62, 159,	2.1-12	124n
22.19	60		171	2.1-6	64
22.28-29	122	29	60, 61	2.1	78
23-27	61, 117n	29.1-5	62, 164,	2.3-10	129, 164,
23-26	61, 102n		171		171
23.1, 27	61	29.2-5, 23		2.6	58
23.5a, 6	102	28, 30	78	2.11-16	129, 164,
23.6	61	29.2-5	62		178
23.25-27	102	29.2,		2.11	64
23.25-26	130n,	3, 19	58	2.17-5.1	64
	131, 164,	29.3-5	59	2.17-18	64
	173	29.6-9	62	3	78
23.25	78	29.9, 22	142n	3.1-5.1	63
24.3	61, 102	29.10-19	62, 159,	5.1	64
24.31	102		169	5.2-7.22	65
25.1	61, 102	29.11-12	157, 159,	5.2-7.10	64
25.6	102		169	5.2-14	63, 64,
26.26	102	29.12	79n		65
26.29-32	102n	29.16	159, 169	5.3	14n
26.30-32	102	29.17	159, 169	5.12-13	142n
27	61, 102n	29.18	159, 169	5.13	164
28-29	62	29.20-22a	62	6	63
28	101	29.20	164, 173	6.1-42	65
28.1-8,		29.22b-25	62	6.1-39	124n
9-10	60	29.23, 25,		6.1-11	64, 129,
28.1-7	60	26	141n		164, 171
28.2-10	126, 129	29.23-24	78	6.5	64
28.2-8	159, 171	29.23	73n	6.5b-6a	129n
28.2	58, 62	29.26-30	62	6.6-11	64
28.3	62	29.28-30	136	6.12-42	64
28.4	62, 141n	29.29	118n	6.14-42	126, 129,
28.5-6	62				160, 169
28.5	73n	*2 Chronicles*		6.16-17	64
28.7-8	101	1.1-17	64	6.16	66
28.7	59, 66,	1.1-7	63	6.18-42	64, 73n
	159, 171	1.1, 15	78	6.36	79n
28.8	61, 62,	1.1	136	6.40-42	160, 169
	159, 171	1.2	141n	7.1-10	63, 64,
28.9-10	85, 159,	1.4	58		65
	171	1.7-13	63, 124n	7.3, 8	141n
28.9	61, 98			7.3	164

INDEX OF AUTHORS

while the other would hold it to b

lso illustrate the important point that
s" of the case in and by themselves, *bu*
ieve their smooth systematization that
stency at issue in such circumstances. In e
ral *partial* perspectives on an over-all se
te and to all appearances mutually inc
e isolated and separate *systematization*
en leads to extrapolation-results which a
patible.[4] Accordingly, it is important (a
g) to recognize that as long as our purporte
he world remains – as it always must – bot
incomplete, this may well exact its price no
ance – that is, in blanks in our knowledge –
consistency.

our knowledge were more synoptic, then (per-
presumably be able to shape a more complex
self-consistent picture, as in the Figure 1 dia-
hus if one line of inquiry addresses itself to the
iological psychology, another to those of be-
hology, inconsistencies of perspective might
t vividly clear picture of the problem is given in John G. Saxe's
Men and the Elephant" Which tells the story of the wise men of
stigated the elephant:

> . . . six men of Indostan,
> To learning much inclined,
> Who went to see the elephant,
> (Though all of them were blind).
> d against the elephant's "broad and sturdy side" and declared the
> y like a wall." Another, who had felt its tusk, pronounced the
> ry like a spear. The third, who took the elephant's tusk, pronounced the
> npared it to a snake; while the fourth, who put his arms around the
> was sure that the animal resembled a tree. A flapping ear convinced
> elephant had the form of a fan; while the sixth blind man was
> had the form of a rope, since he took hold of the tail.

> And so these men of Indostan,
> Disputed loud and long;
> Each in his own opinion
> Exceeding stiff and strong:
> Though each was partly in the right,
> And all were in the wrong.

es the profound lesson of the story of the blind men and the eleph-
sistencies at issue do not result from "the data" available to the men
l and experience. It is their systematizing extension of these data that
onflict.

---

even probably – the case with the present as well.

∴ Our vaunted scientific knowledge does not qualify as authentic knowledge either.

In all due realism it is necessary to adopt the *epistemological Copernicanism* of the second premiss here – a view that rejects the egocentric claim that we ourselves occupy a pivotal position in the epistemic dispensation. We must recognize that there is nothing inherently sacrosanct about our own present cognitive posture *vis-à-vis* that of other, later historical junctures. A kind of intellectual humility is called for – a self-abnegatory diffidence that abstains from the hubris of pretentions to cognitive finality or centrality.

Our attempts at the scientific description and explanation of how things work in the world represents no more than "the very best we can do" at this level of generality and precision and rigor. And we realize in the abstract that it will in due course eventuate that our best is not quite good enough, that our "scientific knowledge" contains an admixture of error. The idea that science does – or sooner or later must – arrive at "the truth of the matter" is not easy to substantiate. There seems no realistic alternative to the supposition that science is wrong – in various ways – and that much of our supposed "knowledge" of the world is a tissue of plausible error. We are thus ill advised to view the science of our own day – or *any* day – as "the final truth of the matter." All we can do is the best we can, the most that can be asked of us in the epistemic circumstances in which we labor. (*Ultra posse. . . .*) There is thus every reason to regard our scientific knowledge as no more than an imperfect estimate, essentially corrigible, subject to revision, inherently uncertain, and liable to be modified or even wholly abandoned in the wake of further scientific innovation.

There is no reason to think that *our* view of things – be it of individual things (the moon, the great wall of China) or of types thereof (the domestic cat, the common cold) – is any more definitive and final than that taken by our own predecessors in the cognitive enterprise. Such an analysis calls for the humbling view that just as we think our predecessors of 100 years ago had a fundamentally inadequate grasp on the furniture of the world, so our successors of 100 years hence will take the same view of *our* knowledge (or purported knowledge) of things. The classical, pre-Kantian view of epistemology embodies a particular approach to things through the contrast between how they appear to us (in terms of our present knowledge or purported knowledge about them) and how they are absolutistically and *an sich* (in terms, say, of God's knowledge about them). The approach taken here exchanges this perspective for one based on the contrast between the *present* view of things and the prospect of an "improved" *future* view of them. It is prepared to dispense with the old-line epistemologists' myth of the God's eye view.

The original Copernican revolution made the point that there is nothing *ontologically* privileged about our own position in space. The doctrine now at issue effectively holds that there is nothing *cognitively* privileged about our own position in time. It urges that *there is nothing epistemically privileged about the present* –ANY present, our own prominently included. Such a perspective indicates not only the incompleteness of "our knowledge" but its presumptive incorrectness as well.

Realism requires us to recognize that, as concerns our scientific understanding of the world, our most secure knowledge is presumably no more than presently accepted error. But this recognition of the fallibilism of our cognitive endeavors must be construed rather as an incentive to do the best we can than an open invitation to scepticism. In human inquiry, the cognitive ideal is correlative with the striving for optimal systematization. And this is an ideal which, like other ideals, is worthy of pursuit, despite the fact that we must realistically recognize that its full attainment lies beyond our grasp.

5. PROBLEMS OF CONSISTENCY

So much for the completeness and correctness of our knowledge. The question of consistency yet remains. For any well develop which a suitably unified psychological theory – were one available – should be able to transcend.) The mere quantitative growth of a scientific field in terms of the ever-mounting proliferation of its literature and its findings may, however, so operate as to preclude such integration.[5] In the actual circumstances of scientific development, even our most valiant efforts may fail to yield a smoothly dovetailed unification.

Indeed, a situation of this sort seems currently to be developing in natural science, as Eugene P. Wigner (Nobel laureate in physics for 1960) has detailed in the following terms:

We now have, in physics, two theories of great power and interest: the theory of quantum phenomena and the theory of relativity. These two theories have their roots in mutually exclusive groups of phenomena. Relativity theory applies to macroscopic bodies, such as stars. The event of coincidence, that is, in ultimate analysis, of collision, is the primitive event in the theory of relativity and defines a point in space-time, or at least would define a point if the colliding particles were infinitely small. Quantum theory has its roots in the microscopic world and, from its point of view, the event of coincidence, or of collision, even if it takes place between particles of no spatial extent, is not primitive and not at all sharply isolated in space-time. The two theories operate with different mathematical concepts – the four dimensional Riemann space and the infinite dimensional Hilbert space, respectively. So far, the two theories could not be united, that is, no mathematical formulation exists to which both of these theories are approximations. All physicists believe that a union of the two theories is inherently possible and that we shall find it. Nevertheless, it is possible also to imagine that no union of the two theories can be found.[6]

[5] In this context, we must not fail to note that the compartmentalization is, after all, a basic aspect of the division of labor achieved by dividing science into branches – a part of the very reason for being of scientific specialization.

[6] Eugene P. Wigner, "The Unreasonable Effectiveness of Mathematics in the Natural Sciences," *Communications on Pure and Applied Mathematics*, vol. 13 (1960),

There is no guarantee that science – as far and as best as we humans can cultivate it – must issue in an account of nature and its workings from which all elements of inconsistency have been excluded.[7] No deity has made an epistemic covenant with us that assures that our science – as it develops in actual practice – must issue in a consistent picture of the world. It is a perfectly real prospect that science might in fact evolve (in a seemingly settled way) into such a Wigner-condition of internal inconsistency. The inevitability of incompleteness and of compartmentalization assures that inconsistency can conceivably prove a real prospect – and indeed one that need not prove to be a merely transient feature of "the presently imperfect state" of the current state of our knowledge, but might well be ultimately ineradicable, affecting every realizable state thereof. One certainly cannot rule out this prospect on any grounds of general principle.[8]

No doubt, one is never absolutely *forced* to accept this sort of inconsistency as irrevocably final and as demanding an ultimate and inescapable sacrifice of the regulative principle at issue. For, as the very nature of the preceding example indicates, the inconsistency at issue can be viewed as "the result of mere incompleteness." We could always tell ourselves in a hopeful tone – "If only we knew a bit more, if only we could push inquiry around the next corner, then we could eliminate the inconsistency presently confronting us; if only our information were enhanced and our science more synoptic, the difficulty would presumably be overcome." But its potential unrealism does not make this line of approach a very satisfying one. Although in theory, one *can* always save the ideal of consistency in this way, the crucial fact remains

pp. 1–14 (see pp. 11–12). Wigner has suggested in private conversation that a more radical disunity is at issue. The space-time metric of general relativity requires mathematically *punctiform* occurrence-configurations, whereas the quantum theory excludes the prospect of such point-events. The requirements of the two domains are to all appearances incompatible with one another.

[7] Cf. the author's *Cognitive Systematization* (Oxford, 1978). The present discussion draws on this work.

[8] The situation is reminiscent of the late nineteenth-century split between physicists (especially William Thompson, later Lord Kelvin) on the one hand and geologists and biologists (especially T. H. Huxley) on the other over the issue of the age of the earth. See the discussion in Stephen G. Brush, "Science and Culture in the Nineteenth Century," *The Graduate Journal*, vol. 7 (1969), pp. 479–565.

that beyond a certain point it would – in practice – become *unreasonable*, nay Quixotic, to do so.[9]

While the totality of what we take ourselves to know is individually and distributively accepted as true, we nevertheless recognize that, holistically and collectively, it must be presumed to contain various (otherwise unidentifiable) errors.[10] And once our recognition of this fact about our knowledge is recognized as part of the corpus of our knowledge itself, the whole veers sharply towards the formally inconsistent. For when we recognize at the level of metabelief that some of our individual beliefs are false, our belief-system as a whole becomes inconsistent.

These deliberations point towards the *Preface Paradox*, which has been formulated by D. C. Makinson in the following terms:

Consider the writer who, in the Preface to his book, concedes the occurrence of errors among his statements. Suppose that in the course of his book a writer makes a great many assertions, which we shall call $s_1, \ldots, s_n$. Given each one of these, he believes that it is true. . . . However, to say that not everything I assert in this book is true, is to say that at least one statement in this book is false. That is to say that at least one of $s_1, \ldots, s_n$ is false, where $s_1, \ldots, s_n$ are the statements in the book; that $(s_1 \& \ldots \& s_n)$ is false; that $\sim(s_1 \& \ldots \& s_n)$ is true. The author who writes and believes each of $s_1, \ldots, s_n$ and yet in a preface asserts and believes $\sim(s_1 \& \ldots \& s_n)$ is, it appears, behaving very rationally. Yet clearly he is holding logically incompatible beliefs: he believes each of $s_1, \ldots, s_n, \sim(s_1 \& \ldots \& s_n)$, which form an inconsistent set. The man is being rational though inconsistent.[11]

[9] Compare to Keith Lehrer, "Reason and Consistency" in idem (ed.), *Analysis and Metaphysics* (Dordrecht, 1975), pp. 57–74.

[10] C. S. Peirce was perhaps the first to remark this circumstance explicitly. He wrote that ". . . while holding certain propositions to be each individually perfectly certain, we may and ought to think it likely that some one of them, if not more, is false." (*Collected Papers*, vol. V, sect. 5.498. Compare Roderick Chisholm, *The Theory of Knowledge* (2nd ed., Englewood Cliffs, 1976), pp. 96–97, for a rather implausible interpretation of this situation.

[11] D. C. Makinson, "The Paradox of the Preface," *Analysis*, vol. 25 (1964), pp. 205–207.

Just this circumstance typifies our cognitive situation. We realize full well *that* the set of assertions comprising "our scientific knowledge" contains errors, but cannot of course say just where these errors lie. With respect to "the body of scientific knowledge of the day" we can apply the distinction between actual knowledge and plausible error only retrospectively, but not contemporaneously.

To be sure, someone might contend that this position is inappropriate – that it is just wrong to accept the Preface Paradox situation at face value. The following argument might be offered here:

> By adding the belief that renders his beliefs inconsistent . . . [one] automatically forgoes the chance of optimum success in the search for truth, that is, believing truths and only truths.[12]

But this objection seems frivolous. Here, as elsewhere, one must recognize that the best is the enemy of the good. We must be realistic, and realistically speaking "the chance of *optimum* success" in a perfectionistic construction of this term is well worth forgoing if its maintenance stands in the way of more realistic and attainable aspirations. It follows from the cognitive Copernicanism that we have no alternative to accepting that we "don't have a snowball's chance in hell" of realizing the goal of believing truths and only truths. The object of the cognitive enterprise is not *this* unworkable idealization, but the achievement of the most favorable balance of truth over error.[13] And given this fact, inconsistency looks far less daunting, seeing that the optimal policy correlative with *this* conception may well call for chancing the prospect of inconsistency.

Admittedly, inconsistency can always be avoided if one is absolutely intent on doing so. It results from accepting too much – the whole of some group of incompatible theses. Inconsistency can thus always be evaded by the simple step of refusing to accept those theses that generate it. Scepticism, the abstention from acceptance, therefore affords a sure-fire

---

[12] Keith Lehrer, *Knowledge* (Oxford, 1974), p. 203.
[13] Compare pp. 144–145 above.

guarantee against inconsistency. But as we have said time and again, the aim of the cognitive enterprise is not just to avoid error but to engross truth. (Nothing ventured, nothing gained!) Now to secure truths we must *accept* something, and to accept something rationally, we must have rules or standards or criteria of acceptance. But if these rules or standards or criteria indicate the acceptability of mutually discordant theses (as they indeed can), then there is something unsatisfying – something too pristine, purist, and ultramundane – about rejecting them *en bloc* simply and solely on this account. No doubt inconsistency is something undesirable and negative, but it is not so horrendous that we should abandon the entire cognitive enterprise rather than run any risk of it.

The key point is that the acceptance of an inconsistency-embracing world-picture is governed by the same basic cognitive standards as the acceptance of *any* such picture – to wit, a cost-benefit calculation using the usual parameters of inductive systematization: evidential strength, rational economy, simplicity, uniformity of treatment, etc. A complex constellation of systematic considerations is at issue, producing a situation in which there can be reciprocal give and take in the mutual adjustment of component elements, a give and take from which even consistency itself is not altogether exempt.

The risk of inconsistency is an ineliminable fact of epistemic life. Its shadow dogs every step of the pursuit of truth. Every theoretical extrapolation from the data runs the risk of clashing head-on with some other. The data themselves may conflict and cry out for theoretical reconciliation. Every expansion of our knowledge through the accession of new data may well contradict some cherished theory. The reach of potential inconsistency is pervasive. We need not welcome this – nor need we make a *virtue* of necessity – but we must accept it. To be sure, we will strive ardently – and doubtless rightly – to eliminate inconsistency insofar as possible. But there is not, and cannot be, any theoretical advance guarantee that this struggle must succeed and that all inconsistency can ultimately be eliminated from the arena of our cognitive endeavors. Nor need these endeavors be abandoned on that account. The very aims and objectives of the cognitive enterprise – above all, completeness and systematic comprehensiveness – constrain the risk of inconsistency upon us. Unquestionably, no sensible person would court inconsistency for its own sake. But this is not the issue. The point is that one can reasonably be in a position of tolerating inconsistencies – and quite reasonably so – when driven to it by the natural operation of the (otherwise defensible) principles that govern the conduct of our cognitive affairs.[14]

6. CONCLUSION

As the preceding deliberations indicate, the body of what we purport as "knowledge" is gravely defective, exhibiting deficiencies in such fundamental respects as completeness, correctness, and even consistency. These lines of thought point inexorably to the conclusion that there is a substantial element of truth to the sceptic's complaints against the adequacy of our purported knowledge.

To begin with, the sceptic is quite right on the issue of the demanding absolutism of knowledge. When something is claimed as known it is indeed thereby claimed to be certain, exact, incorrigible, etc. And this absolutism – however "realistically" construed – makes the substantiation of knowledge claims a relatively demanding enterprise. (To be sure, the sceptic is wrong to inflate these difficulties into impossibilities, construing the absolutes at issue in an unrealistic and hyperbolic sense which quite improperly loads the argument decisively in his favor from the very outset.) Again, the sceptic is right in his assault against foundationalism and the idea of absolutely certain irrefrangible premises on which the whole structure of objective factual knowledge can be erected. He is right in contending that insofar as such absolutely secure data are available to us through the phenomenal certainties of immediate experience, they cannot yield *objective* knowledge. Moreover, the sceptic is right in his insistence on the "evidential gap" as a fact of life that assures the theo-

[14] The ideas of this section are developed more fully in Nicholas Rescher and Robert Brandom, *The Logic of Inconsistency* (Oxford, 1979).

retical fallibility of all objective factual claims. These must – in view of their very objectivity – inevitably be such that their assertive content transcends the supportive data we can ever secure on their behalf. The sceptic is also right in holding that what we vaunt as our "scientific knowledge" must always be conceived of as containing a substantial admixture of error. (To be sure, scepticism goes too far in construing such a concession of fallibility as to destroy any and all prospects of the realization of knowledge.) Finally, the sceptic is right that we cannot claim the completeness or the correctness and indeed not even the consistency of "our knowledge" of the world.

In sum, the sceptic is right on virtually the entire gamut of the subsidiary issues regarding the inadequacy of our knowledge. He has fought a stiff fight and has won many battles in its course.

Nevertheless, the sceptic has lost the war. For he is wrong in regarding the nature of knowledge as being so absolutistic that any and all prospects of warranted claims to its attainment are in principle unrealizable. And he is quite wrong in maintaining that all avenues towards rationally warranted knowledge claims are blocked by any recognition of their theoretical defeasibility. Most importantly, the sceptic is wrong in holding that the presumptive incompleteness, potential incorrectness, and possible inconsistency of "our knowledge" so operate as to block any prospect of our advancing legitimate claims to the possession of knowledge.

The sceptic is nevertheless quite correct in his analysis of the *collective* (global) shortcomings of our purported knowledge – he is quite correct in insisting that it must be recognized and acknowledged that – at the generic, wholesale level of metacognitive consideration – what we confidently acclaim as "our knowledge" has various significant flaws, seeing that it is patently incomplete, probably incorrect, and very possibly even inconsistent. But his analysis of the implications of this situation is profoundly mistaken. For the sceptic makes the mistake of thinking that this *global* fact has decisively negative *local* implications in providing a macrolevel basis for rejecting knowledge at the microlevel of particularized claims. The sceptic illicitly visits the flaws of the collective whole upon the distributive parts, rejecting all particularized claims as specifically doubtful (S-doubtful) on the basis of such general considerations (of G-doubtfulness). And this line of reasoning is – as we have seen – quite improper.

It must be conceded to the sceptic that even when we are *rationally entitled* to claim to know something, matters may yet still so eventuate that we do not *actually know* this – that we must eventually retract and grant, with the wisdom of hindsight, the falsity of our knowledge-claim and perhaps that of the purported fact as well. And one must concede that we do not *really* know various things that we not only *think* we know, but even *appropriately* think we know (albeit, of course, not *correctly*). The sceptic's key mistake lies in his belief that such concessions can be exploited to invalidate the propriety of our knowledge claims in general and to impugn the whole of the cognitive enterprise.

With all due respect to the Hegelian view of understanding according to which "nothing can be known rightly without knowing all else rightly,"[15] we must insist that this stance makes the sceptic's life too easy. One need not know everything to know anything: our getting *something* wrong does not entail our getting *everything* wrong pervasively. The concession that "the body of our knowledge" contains various errors and deficiencies does not make it in order to withdraw each and every one of the particular claims to knowledge that lie within its precincts.

Yet the sceptic has certainly not struggled in vain. Much essential clarification of the nature of knowledge can only be attained by analyzing how the key arguments deployed by the sceptic fail in the final analysis to establish his governing conclusion of the illegitimacy of claims to knowledge. What the sceptic's argumentation has managed to achieve is not to establish the unattainability of knowledge but to exhibit the inherent limitations of such knowledge as we can properly lay claim to. In this way, the sceptic has – no doubt to his own discomfiture – rendered a highly useful and constructive service to the cognitivist position.

[15] Bernard Bosanquet, *Logic* (2 vols., 2nd ed., London, 1911), p. 393. Cf. Hegel's *Science of Logic* (London, 1929), tr. W. H. Johnstone and L. G. Struthers, vol. II, §257; p. 242.

Appendix

FORMAL ASPECTS OF KNOWLEDGE

This appendix gathers together for convenient overview the discussions of various aspects of the "formal logic" of knowledge scattered through various places in the body of the book.[1]

Table 1 begins by summarizing some clearly valid principles of the logic of knowledge.

Table 1

Some Patently Valid Principles of the "Logic" of Knowledge

(1) *The Veracity of Knowledge* [a]
$\vdash Kxp \rightarrow p$

(2) *The Consistency of Knowledge* [b]
$\vdash (Kxp \mathbin{\&} Kxq) \rightarrow \text{compat}(p, q)$

(3) *Modus Ponens for Knowledge* [c]
$\vdash (Kxp \mathbin{\&} Kx[p \rightarrow q]) \rightarrow Kxq$

(4) *The Decomposibility of Conjunctive Knowledge*
$\vdash Kx(p \mathbin{\&} q) \rightarrow (Kxp \mathbin{\&} Kxq)$

(5) *The Irrefutability of Knowledge* [d]
$\vdash Kxp \rightarrow Kx \sim (\exists q)(q \mathbin{\&} [q \rightarrow \sim p])$

Notes:

(a) See Section 1 of Chap. II.

(b) See Section 1 of Chap. II. Note that (2) is an immediate consequence of (1), and could indeed be strengthened by changing the second occurrence of 'x' to 'y'. Note too that compat(p, q) must be construed to entail, *inter alia*, that $\sim (p \rightarrow \sim q)$.

(c) See Section 1 of Chap. II.

(d) See p. 114.

---

[1] The reader interested in the systematic development of the formal logic of the knowledge-operator K should consult the essay "On Alternatives in Epistemic Logic" in the author's *Studies in Modality* (Oxford, 1974; *American Philosophical Quarterly* Monograph No. 8).

It should be noted from the very outset that epistemic theory cannot concern itself with the "formal logic" of *occurrent* knowledge – with what someone does actually and actively *heed* within his range of active and explicit attention – because such a concept is too psychologically and biographically oriented. Nor yet does it deal with person-relatively *dispositional* knowledge in the sense of a person's individual inclinations to give assent. For this too leaves room for biographical and psychological idiosyncrasies to engender something too variable to possess a formal structure of the sort with which epistemological theorizing can profitably deal. Nor does the theory deal with merely *putative* knowledge, for otherwise principle (1) would clearly be inappropriate.

The conception of "knowledge" at issue in these epistemological discussions is accordingly *latent* knowledge of the truth, where "Kxp" is to be construed to mean that p lies within x's "stock of knowledge" – the knowledge that x "has at his disposal," realistically speaking, the knowledge that he could reasonably be expected to realize actively and occurrently with effort and a bit of luck. And this must be so construed as to focus our concern upon what a person "can" bring to explicit and occurrent awareness in the realistic sense of this term "can," as reflecting an ability-to-do, a determinable skill or capacity on the basis of which reasonable expectations can be formed.

Moreover, we must presuppose that the individuals at issue in the range of our variables are *minimally* rational persons, that is, persons who can safely be assumed always to make at least the most basic and rudimentary inferences from their knowledge. (For only thus would principle (3), for example, be forthcoming.) Acceptance of (3) also commits us to the idea that if the immediate inference $p \rightarrow q$ is something so *utterly obvious* and simple-minded that "it's safe to assume that *everybody* knows it," then the inference from Kxp to Kxq can safely be postulated. Since it seems unproblematically plausible to class the implication from p & q to p (and to q) as "utterly obvious" in the aforementioned sense, we obtain (4) as a consequence of (3). Again, once we suppose that *any* rational person knows that the truth of a thesis is incompatible with that of any thesis that is incompatible with it – that is, knows that $p \rightarrow \sim(\exists q)(q \,\&\, [q \rightarrow \sim p])$ – then we obtain (5) through the mediation of (3).

Going beyond the "patently valid" principles of Table 1, we come to certain other principles that seen relatively plausible. These are summarized in Table 2.

Table 2

Some Plausible Principles of the "Logic" of Knowledge

(6) *The Conjunctivity of Knowledge* [a]

    $(Kxp \,\&\, Kxq) \rightarrow Kx(p \,\&\, q)$

(7) *The KK-Thesis: Knowing Entails Knowing One Knows* [b]

    $Kxp \rightarrow KxKxp$

Notes:

(a) See Section 1 of Chap. II.

(b) See Section 5 of Chap. VI.

These principles, though plausible, are nevertheless a bit more problematic than the preceding ones in that they introduce somewhat more powerful assumptions about x's capacity to conjure with the materials found within his "stock of knowledge." The first principle implies that a person can reach into this stock to make proper combinations. And the second is more questionable yet. It turns heavily on the supposition that a person can potentially bring whatever he knows to explicit and occurrent awareness. These principles thus indicate further the "latency" that is at issue.

From the logician's point of view, it should be noted that the "logic" of knowledge in the sense of the preceding discussion could be axiomatized by supplementing propositional logic with a knowledge operator K subject to a modest handful of basic stipulations. We would begin with the

Definition

$\models P$ iff $(\forall x)KxP$.

Note that $\models$ represents the "utter obviousness" of that which "any rational person can safely be presumed to realize." And we would now adopt the following

Axioms

A1 $Kxp \rightarrow p$

A2 $(Kxp \,\&\, Kx[p \rightarrow q]) \rightarrow Kxq$

A3 $(Kxp \,\&\, Kxq) \rightarrow Kx(p \,\&\, q)$

A4 $Kxp \rightarrow KxKxp$

A5 $\models (p \,\&\, q) \rightarrow p$

A6 $\models (p \,\&\, q) \rightarrow q$

A7 $\models p \rightarrow \,\sim(\exists q)\,(q \,\&\, [q \rightarrow \,\sim p])$

All the principles of Tables 1 and 2 can readily be derived on this basis (as we have, in effect, already observed). Note that these axioms fall into two groups: (1) those regarding the mechanics of the knowledge operator K itself, namely A1–A4, and (2) those relating to special stipulations regarding "what it is safe to assume that everybody knows," namely A5–A7, which represent supplementary suppositions that enable us to implement A2. This second list could doubtless be extended without encountering lesser plausibilities than those already at issue in A5–A7. (For example, $\models (p \,\&\, [p \rightarrow q]) \rightarrow q$ would doubtless be a candidate.) In this regard, no claims to finality or completeness can be made on behalf of the given set of axioms. On the other hand, however, the various standard systems of epistemic logic are undoubtedly too liberal in this respect. For they generally involve a commitment to logical omniscience, in postulating a universal

---

Table 3

Some Principles of the Modal "Logic" of Knowledge

Definitions: (i) $\Diamond_x p \;\; = Df \;\; (\forall q)(Kxq \supset \text{compat}(p, q))$

(ii) $\Box_x p \;\; = Df \;\; \sim \Diamond_x \sim p = (\exists q)(Kxq \,\&\, [q \rightarrow p])$

(8) *The Known is "Epistemically Necessary"*[a]

   $Kxp \rightarrow \Box_x p$

(9) *A Real (or "Epistemic") Possibility of Falsehood Defeats Knowledge*[a]

   $\Diamond_x \sim p \rightarrow \,\sim Kxp$

Note:

(a) The principles of this table are discussed in Section 3 of Chap. VII.

recognition of all the truths of propositional logic or even of the truths of logic in general.[2] Such an approach treats the issue of latent knowledge – of what a person "can" bring to explicit and occurrent awareness – in too generous a sense.

The acceptable principles at issue in Tables 1 and 2 can be further amplified by introducing certain modal ideas into the "logic" of knowledge. This is done in Table 3. The principles at issue in this table obtain on logical grounds alone, subject to the given definitions of the modal operations $\Diamond$ and $\Box$.

Some clearly unacceptable principles of the "logic" of knowledge are set out in Table 4.

Table 4
Some Patently Unacceptable (Pseudo) Principles of the "Logic" of Knowledge

(i) *Logical Omniscience*[a]

$$\dashv (Kxp \ \& \ ([p \rightarrow q]) \rightarrow Kxq$$

And even the weaker version of the principle

If $\vdash p$, then Kxp

is unacceptable.

(ii) *The Defeat of Knowledge by a Mere Possibility of Error*[b]

$$\dashv \Diamond \sim p \rightarrow \ \sim Kxp$$

or equivalently

$$Kxp \rightarrow \Box p$$

(iii) *Ominiscience re. Ignorance*[c]

$$\dashv \ \sim Kxp \rightarrow Kx \sim Kxp$$

Notes:

(a) See Section 1 of Chap. II and Section 4 of Chap. III. Note that the weaker version follows from the fact that a $\vdash$-theorem is derivable from any assertion whatsoever.

(b) See Section 3 of Chap. VII and cf. pp. 133–139.

(c) See Section 6 of Chap. VI.

Since compat(p, q) must be construed to yield $\sim (p \rightarrow \sim q)$, we have it from thesis (2) of Table 1 that

$$(Kxp \ \& \ Kxq) \rightarrow \ \sim (p \rightarrow \sim q)$$

[2] See the author's "On Alternatives in Epistemic Logic" (*op. cit.*).

which leads at once to:

$$(Kxp \ \& \ [p \rightarrow q]) \rightarrow \ \sim Kx \sim q.$$

A consequence of what one knows is certainly something that "is so for all that one knows." But the unacceptable thesis (i) of Table 4 of course makes a much stronger claim in asserting that this is something one actually knows to be so. Observe, too, that (i) is equivalent with

$$([p \rightarrow q] \ \& \ \sim Kxq) \rightarrow \ \sim Kxp.$$

It would thus place a most powerful weapon at the sceptic's disposal. A claim to knowledge of a fact would now be defeated by the lack of knowledge of even a single one of its implications, making possible the defeat of knowledge through lack of knowledge of even a single consequence of a purportedly known thesis. (Cp. p. 96 above.)

Moreover, the unacceptable principle (ii) blocks the prospect of any contingent knowledge. Principle (iii), on the other hand, militates unfairly in the opposite direction. It makes the cognitivists' task too simple in transmuting ignorance into knowledge. (See p. 118 above.)

Note that if the "knowledge" at issue in our discussion were *virtual* knowledge – that is, dealt with what *can in theory* be deduced (by anybody) from what a person "knows" in some more actualistic and occurrent sense of the term, then principle (i) of Table 4 would indeed obtain.[3] But the *latent* knowledge actually at issue in our present analysis does not meet this condition. It deals with what a person "can *in (realistic) practice*" extract from his stock of knowledge, not with what he "can *in theory*" extract. While this idea of "virtual knowledge" is exactly what is at issue with the epistemic necessity operator □ of Table 3, it does not answer to the "knowledge" to which our principal deliberations are addressed.

It warrants note that these unacceptable principles result from acceptable ones by the process we have designated as "inflation of the consequences" (see pp. 53–54 above).

---

[3] Particularly since thesis (6) of Table 2 enables us always to combine various known items into one grand conjunction to serve as the known antecedent here.

This involves an improper shift by which the consequent of a valid principle is illicitly strengthened, the move from $\Box\,(Kxp \to p)$ to $Kxp \to \Box p$ being a paradigm example. (Compare Sect. 3 of Chap. IV.) Thus, for example, compare thesis (i) of Table 4 with thesis (3) of Table 1; thesis (ii) of Table 4 with thesis (8) of Table 3; and thesis (iii) of Table 4 with the innocuous $\sim Kxp \to \sim KxKxp$.

Some further plausible-seeming but unacceptable principles arise in the context of quantification. Thus consider the two theses:

(iv) $Kx(\forall q)C(q) \to (\forall q)KxC(q)$

(v) $(\forall q)KxC(q) \to Kx(\forall q)C(q)$.

Neither of these is tenable. To see this with (iv), let the condition $C(q)$ be simply $q \to q$, to yield

$$Kx(\forall q)(q \to q) \to (\forall q)Kx(q \to q).$$

The antecedent is plausible enough: a rational knower presumably knows that all propositions are self-entailing. But one will hesitate to say of *every* proposition that the knower at issue knows that *it* specifically entails itself, since many propositions will be altogether beyond his cognitive ken (for example, those dealing with people and places he knows not of).

To see the untenability of (v) consider the following example. Let the domain of a quantification at issue consist of all propositions considered (affirmed or denied) in a certain book. And let $C(q)$ obtain if and only if q is about dogs. Then the antecedent of (v) comes to: "Of any and every one of the propositions at issue (say those asserted or denied in that specific book), x knows that it is about dogs." But the consequent of (v) comes to "x knows that all the propositions at issue (all those considered in the book) are about dogs." And this consequence may not obtain. Even though x knows of each book-member that it has the property ϕ, he may not know all book-members have ϕ since he may well not realize that his survey of book-members is actually complete.

In the establishment of a "logic" of knowledge due caution must thus be exercised to exclude *formal* principles that are not ultimately tenable. But it is of course also possible to make mistaken assumptions about *material* principles. Let us consider an example of this.

The pivotal argumentation of Peter Unger's recent book *Ignorance: A Case for Scepticism* (Oxford, 1975) runs essentially as follows. Let "*Dxp*" abbreviate "*x* is being deceived by an evil demon (wicked scientist, or what have you) into accepting *p* (wrongly and on inadequate grounds)." Consider now the following line of reasoning (as reconstructed from p. 15 of Unger's discussion):[4]

1. $Kxp \rightarrow \sim Dxp$ (an "evident" epistemological truth)
2. $Kx(Kxp \rightarrow \sim Dxp)$ (a rudimentary assumption about *x*, viz., that he recognizes the "evident" truth at issue in step 1)
3. $Kxp \rightarrow KxKxp$ (the KK-thesis)
4. Suppose: Kxp
5. $KxKxp$ from 3 and 4
6. $Kx \sim Dxp$ from 2, 5 by the principle: $(Kxp \ \& \ Kx[p \rightarrow q]) \rightarrow Kxq$
7. $Kxp \rightarrow Kx \sim Dxp$ from steps 4–6
8. $\sim (\exists p)Kx \sim Dxp$ (a purported fact of epistemic life)
9. $\sim (\exists p)Kxp$ from 7 and 8

The one place where this otherwise cogent argumentation goes amiss is at step 8, the premissed contention that "We can never know that we aren't being tricked by the evil demon." We of course *do* know that such demonological assumptions can be dismissed in various concrete uses. They lie outside the range of *realistic* possibilities that must be reckoned with in the sphere of our cognitive concerns. To insist flatly that we don't know this sort of thing is again to succumb to the sceptic's favorite device of "inflating the consequences" – in moving from the fact that it is *hypothetically* possible that such exotic circumstances obtain to the conclusion that this is *realistically* possible and therefore knowledge-impeding. The mistake in this argumentation does not lie in its formal structure but in its material assumptions.

[4] The "reconstruction" at issue is designed to achieve the desideratum of rendering the argument at issue formally (i.e. deductively) valid.

Index of Names

Subject Index